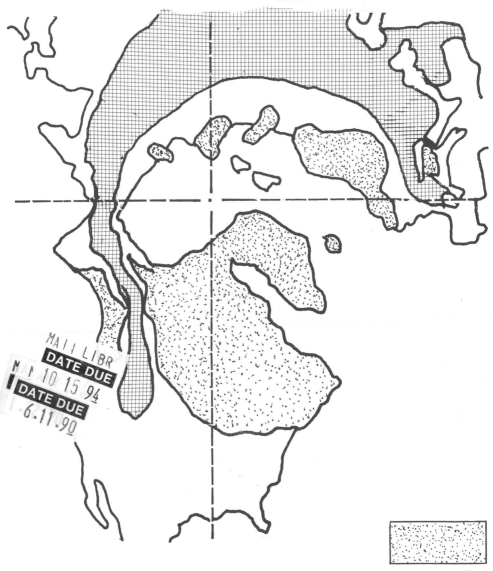

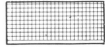

ICE EXTENSION

OCCUPIED AREAS

extension and archeological complex areas over Eurasia and North
nerica, 30,000 B.P.

DOGS
of the
AMERICAN
INDIANS

WILLIAM PFERD III

Edited by
William W. Denlinger and R. Annabel Rathman

Cover Design by
Bob Groves

DENLINGER'S PUBLISHERS, LTD.
Box 76, Fairfax, Virginia 22030

Library of Congress Cataloging-in-Publication Data

Pferd, William, 1922-1987
    Dogs of the American Indians.

    Bibliography: p.
    1. Indians of North America—Domestic animals.
2. Indians—Domestic animals. 3. Dogs—North America—History.
4. Dogs—America—History. 5. Dog breeds—North America—History.
6. Dog breeds—America—History. I. Denlinger, William Watson.
II. Rathman, R. Annabel.   III. Title.
E98.D67P44   1987   636.7'008997   87-432
ISBN 0-87714-126-6

International Standard Book Number: 0-87714-126-6

Preface

The pleasure of dogs for Americans is everywhere, and so it has been for many thousands of years. Ever since the first Paleo-Indians entered the North American Continent from Asia across the Bering Strait, there has been a strong, continuous, and vital relationship between dog and man. Individual dogs or packs of dogs have served as companions or aides to the children, the wives, and the menfolk of all classes during all periods of our history. This book presents the history of the dogs of the American Indians from prehistoric times to the late 1800s.

The story of the American Indian dog is inexorably tied to the story of the tribal groups, exploring bands, pioneer settlers, farmers, and landed gentry that have occupied the American Continents. But what evidence do we have to show the origin and history in the Americas of this friend of man? The answer will lead the reader into many fields. Archeology, literature, art, and the lore of times when the American Indians ruled the continents, when we were a colonial power, a new nation—all contain facts about the Indian dog. The writings of the famous explorers, pioneers, and founding fathers are a source of fascinating glimpses of their thoughts and actions about these dogs. Artists from the eighteenth century permit the identification of different native breeds from the time of the early settlements. The earliest of dog books printed in the Americas are a mine of facts, while the writings of scientists who went to meet the aboriginal tribes or to unearth their remains provide a wealth of information about prehistoric and Indian dogs.

Although during the centuries before the American Revolution important social events were the major reasons for leaving a written record, one is pleasantly surprised at how frequently there appear words about dogs in the writings. Fortunately, it was a time when an extensive correspondence was accepted as normal, when diaries were fashionable, and when having an original painting was within the means of many a landowner or merchant. Contained in many of these documents are descriptions of the varieties of dogs in early America, and pictured in the works of art are the dogs of the Indians.

I have searched assiduously among the writings of the famous and not so famous explorers, missionaries, and pioneers to glean the references to dogs that are the basis of this book. The works of artists from the eighteenth century permit us to identify likenesses of the different types of dogs before and after the American Revolution. They help us to understand the descriptions of the various Indian dogs that appear in the books that were published during this time. Many of the famous early explorers were dog fanciers and have left us accounts of Indian dogs in the reports of their treks across the American Continents. And lastly, a variety of scientists from Britain and America have gone afield to meet the aboriginal tribes or to unearth their remains and, in the process, provide information about the prehistoric era and the dog.

I have attempted to provide in this book a single source for all known references to the varieties of Indian dogs. I have excerpted from original sources those portions that provide information about "the Indian's best friend," omitting parts that are too dated or in gross error when judged by modern standards. The numerous prints and pictures also are from the originals of the period so that you can judge with the artist's eye, conformation, type, and style of the early American breeds.

After considerable thought about how to organize the material—by source books, or by famous owners of special dogs or breeds—I have decided to present a number of chapters dealing with identifiable Indian dogs. The work describes all known types of Indian dogs or breeds. Both the serious student of dogs and the fancier of a single breed will find enjoyment in identifying, from among the varieties of dogs that roamed the Indian villages and territories, the early American cousins of their favorite pet. Of course, all who are interested in the American Indian will find here things of special interest that are omitted from the conventional books about their history. Included are the vibrant activities and courageous deeds of living men, women, and children: the natives of the American Continents—and their favored dogs.

The work reflects the comments and suggestions for greater clarity made by Dr. Brenda F. Beebe, Department of Anthropology, University of Toronto, and Frank A. Norrick, Principal Museum Anthropologist, Lowie Museum of Anthropology, University of California, Berkeley. These eminent anthropologists and experts in Indian history have generously contributed their time and attention toward improving the work. I wish to express my gratitude for their efforts.

Finally, my special thanks are extended to Annabel Rathman for her good cheer, care, and efficiency in editing the manuscript, and to my wonderful wife, Jane, for waiting patiently for the end of yet another of my avocational endeavors.

William Pferd III

Contents

Introduction   7
    Coming Together   12
    Man's Best Friend   17
The Historical Record   21
    Dog, Wolf, or Coyote?   27
    Dating the Find   33
Old and New World Dogs   39
    Jaguar Cave Dog   44
    Koster Farm Dog   48
    Port au Choix Dog   49
Dogs in Rock Art   55
    Prehistoric Varieties   60
American Indians and Their Dogs   71
    Breeds of Indian Dogs   74
Great Plains Dogs   79
    Plains-Indian Dog   79
    Sioux Dog   86
Arctic Dogs   99
    Eskimo Dog   99
Sub-Arctic Dogs   115
    Malamute   115
    Hare-Indian Dog   118
Northwest Coast Dogs   125
    Short-legged Indian Dog   125
    Larger or Common Indian Dog   128
    Small Indian Dog   134
    Klamath-Indian Dog   136
    Clallam-Indian Dog   139
Southwest Dogs   143
    Short-nosed Indian Dog   143
    Long-haired Pueblo Dog   145
    Mexican Hairless Dog   148
Inca Indian Dogs   153
    Inca Dog   153
    Long-haired Inca Dog   154
Southern South American Dogs   159
    Peruvian Pug-nosed Dog   159
    Patagonian Dog   160
    Fuegian Dog   162
War Dogs from Europe   169
Tale's End   179
Bibliography   186
Index   190

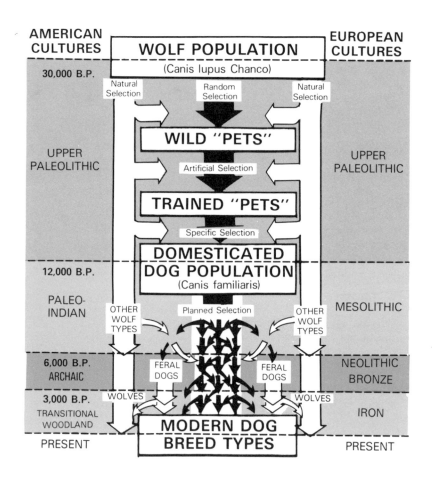

A graphic representation of the development of the dog in North America.

Introduction

It was only about thirty thousand years ago that wild creatures of the plains and forests roamed free on the North and South American Continents. Through an endless series of days and nights the forces of natural selection had shaped a gathering of plants and animals that lived from ocean to ocean and arctic to tropic in total balance and interdependency. Over the prior eons, any change in plant or animal form as it occurred was tested by the natural environment. It might be sustained long enough to permit propagation of a new variant or species, or it might succumb and be lost forever. Through this natural process, the American land masses were, in time, completely occupied by a vast indigenous array of plants and wild animals.

Prior to the decline of the last ice age, into this land of mindless nature, came two new species that would, together with changes in climate, upset the native balance and alter forever the primeval state. It is now clear that these two new entrants on the American scene came from Asia over a connecting land bridge in the far northwest. Remnants of their passage have been found in northwest Alaska along the streams and rivers that flow into the Bering Sea, north of Nome, in the favored valleys and coastal harbors of California, and at sheltered cave sites in the interior of the great Western Plateau region. Even the impressions of the feet of these earliest invaders have been found in the now hardened clay that borders beach areas of the Pacific Ocean. Together, they changed the face of North America: these two companions—man and his dog!

There is abundant evidence of the passage of Mongoloid family groups east and southward across the continent to the Atlantic Ocean and finally to the furthermost southern tip of South America. Archeological remains show a gradual movement over a few thousand years until they totally occupied the land of the Americas. Their arrival and subsequent impact on the natural environment was momentous, for man was the ultimate predator. Man came first as destroyer in search for the means of survival, and later as builder, altering the environment of which man was soon to become the dominant species.

In many ways, this entrance of man and dog into America can be compared to the momentous incursion some thirty thousand years later when a new violent period of alteration began with the arrival of European settlers. During the intervening thousands of years, man and dog had developed into a variety of groups and types. Man, in tribal bands and cultural groups, regarded dog as his most valuable possession.

Landings on the eastern shores by early explorers from Europe began another period of change. This newest invasion of people with their dogs once again brought great conflict to the American scene, and a whole new set of relationships between man and nature was destined to evolve.

What common threads bind together these two invasions into America of men and their dogs? Were both in search of means to survive? Were both seeking new wealth? Were both drawn by the lure of new adventure? While the Mongoloid hunter-gatherer groups expanded their range in a struggle to partake of nature's bounty, the European explorers and settlers brought a calculating purpose to their efforts. Both groups were responding to the need for survival, for wealth, for excitement, and for better conditions to be hoped for in a new and undeveloped land. While both groups had common aims, so too did they bring common companions and aides—their dogs.

Therefore, to understand the place of the dog in early America, it is necessary to know the nature and conditions of the people that lived in past periods. Since Indians, explorers, settlers, farm and city folk, all play a part in the history, it is necessary to know something of each individual life style in order to understand the place of the dog in this long sweep of time. The story of the dog in America is tied intimately to the tribal groups, exploring bands, lone hunters, and family groups who lived and fought over this vast continent. Dogs have been ever present, as individuals or in packs, serving as either friends or enemies to the children, men, and wives, in all classes and groups of inhabitants.

What evidence do we have to show the origin and history of this friend and sometime foe of man? The answer to such a question leads the researcher into many fields beyond the dog world and, so too, the reader will learn a bit about art and archeology, law and literature as related to the dog and his or her owner. The evidence is often found in odd places and at times requires conjecture and logic to develop its full meaning. Once the search begins, it soon becomes clear that man and dog have been exceptionally close. Wherever there is a record of man, no matter how small or fragmentary, there is usually a surprisingly clear picture or reference to the dog. Wherever there is a record of dog, it includes actions of men who inhabit positions from the lowest to the highest in society and from the least to most educated in the land. Was the dog with the first nomadic hunters who entered the continent? Was he regarded as a thing of value by the early American Indian? Was he a passenger on the ships that carried over the seas the daring Spanish, French, and English explorers? Was he prized by European early settlers? Is his wide acceptance, even today in America, the modern expression of a fundamental relationship? We shall see that there is an ample record to answer these and many other questions and that the answers will show dog and man always together in wonderful and meaningful ways.

Our understanding of the earliest aboriginal dogs is gleaned from the bones uncovered at various archeological digs and from the paintings and writings of explorers and scientists who first visited the American Indians. From the early archeological evidence we know that the dog spread over the Americas along with the various hunting groups and developed into almost as many distinct varieties as there were cultural groups. By the time of the arrival of the European explorers, there were as many as twenty physically different breeds of aboriginal dogs in North and South America. Of course, these breeds have disappeared, except for the Mexican Chihuahua, the Alaskan Malamute, and the Eskimo Dog. Even these remaining three have been changed in appearance by modern dog breeders; of the others, there are only skeletal remains.

What must be considered one of the earliest of American domesticated dogs is an animal known as the Jaguar Cave Dog from Buck Creek Valley, Lemhi County, Idaho, that was uncovered by a team of archeologists led by Dr. Hind Sadek-Kooros in 1962. Actually, the skeletal remains of two distinct breeds of different sizes, discovered at the Jaguar Cave site, have been dated by carbon-14 measurements to about 10,400 B.P. The first dogs found were small, similar in size to terriers of modern times. Later, skull and jawbone fragments of large dogs were found at the same level. These show that the animals probably were similar in form to the Eskimo Dog. The presence of two such differing breeds at the same prehistoric site is positive evidence that considerable attention had been given to the breeding of dogs for thousands of years. Variation in size is one of the pronounced results of domestication, and in this instance indicates that at least two quite different breeds of dogs either came from Asia with the first nomads to pass through Alaska or were the result of a breeding program managed during prior years by the first Americans.

The question of the exact place and time of the emergence of the original dog still remains a mystery. There may, in fact, have been more than one center of dog domestication and possibly at different times. Yet the questions may be nearing an answer. With some feeling of certainty because of new work by anthropologists during recent years, the place of origin of the modern dog is thought to be Tibet. New research by Stanley

J. Olsen and John W. Olsen of the University of Arizona suggests that the small Chinese wolf might be the ancestor of the North American dogs.

During aboriginal times, the domesticated dog served some tribes as food but was also in general use as a pack animal, an aide in hunting, or was kept for pleasure or to provide warmth. For many tribes, dog meat remained a highly regarded addition to any meal, even until the time of the European explorers and settlers. The diary kept by a Canadian trapper in relatively modern times, as recorded by the Reverend John Bachman in a portion of his text for Audubon's *Imperial Collection of Quadrupeds of North America,* gives a vivid and, to some, a mouthwatering picture of a dinner including dog meat. Bachman tells how the trapper's Indian wife cooked a meal of "5 Indian dogs, bear, beaver, mountain cat and raccoon, boiled in bear's grease and mixed with huckleberries." This no doubt was ordinary and delicious fare for many a man and woman in the wilderness and certainly was the sort of meal enjoyed by the first people to inhabit North America.

The earliest European explorers and trappers of the new world, starting with the Spaniards, not only took their favorite dogs with them, but also used and returned home with new and exotic varieties that were obtained from the Indians. These groups of settlers (such as the people in the seventeen ships that Christopher Columbus led in September 1493 on his second voyage of exploration and colonization to the West Indies) took with them a variety of live animals, including a number of large dogs for protection. The first dogs from Europe to touch on the soil of the North American Continent swam ashore from the boats of Hernando de Soto. Landing south of what is now known as Tampa Bay, Florida, in May 1539, with a force of one thousand men, de Soto set off on the exploration of Florida and the southeast region with three hundred fifty horses and a considerable number of guard and hunting dogs. We know for certain that there were large Greyhounds, since it is reported that during the crossing from Spain, a "greyhound fell overboard and swam for five days before one of the following ships came close enough for rescue." Large Mastiffs and Spanish Hounds, similar to the Podenco Espagnol and the Braco Navarro, the ancestors of all pointing dogs, were companions and aides to explorers and kept the Indians in check during the many skirmishes led by Columbus and de Soto.

By the time European explorers reached the Americas, Indian dogs were widespread over the two continents, from Alaska in the far north to Tierra del Fuego at the tip of South America. There were many large varieties, including the Eskimo sled dog, at least eight varieties of medium-sized dogs, and at least five different varieties of small dogs.

Alas, all have disappeared, or have been greatly altered, under the pressure from European immigrants. The introduction of European breeds brought more highly trained and cultivated types to the American scene. They were sought out by the native American Indians and judged to be superior to their own indigenous varieties. It was only where very special needs were served by particular breed types that the Indian dog survived. At the time of the discovery of America, there existed in Europe fourteen distinct varieties, as identified by Juliana Berners in her 1487 manuscript titled *The Boke of St. Albans.* By the time of the landing of de Soto, the number of breeds worthy of identification had grown to more than twenty-two in Europe. This was recorded in 1576 by Johannes Caius, Doctor of Medicine at the University of Cambridge, in his renowned work, *Of English Dogges, the Diversities, the Names, the Nature and the Properties.*

It is interesting to compare the European varieties with the native American types. While both groups developed independently over at least a thirty thousand year period, from perhaps the same ancestral stock, both apparently had expanded by the sixteenth century to include a similar number of varieties and sizes. In Europe, the larger types, called *Venatici,* included hounds that excelled in scenting game and giving chase. The middle-sized groups were *Aucupatori* that sought the bird and showed its flight by pursuit. The smallest type, called *Delicatus,* included toy dogs to satisfy the desires of "dainty dames" and were carried about for pleasure and to warm the hands. A fourth group, called *Rustici,* were of various sizes, depending on their purpose, such as to shepherd flocks, to defend property, or to operate the turnspit.

Both continents had their varieties of large, medium, and small dogs, and in about equal numbers. Nevertheless, the impact of the European dogs on their American cousins was disastrous. Cast in a superior role and just as their European masters displaced the American Indians, the dogs from Europe slowly dominated their American counterparts and helped cause their extinction in a few hundred years. The slow evolution and diversification that had produced a variety of types in great abundance across the land was ended suddenly.

But let us turn the pages of time back through the years to the period when the small wild wolves that are the main ancestors to all dogs were running in packs alongside that other species that lived naturally in social groups. Man's behavior patterns and those of wolves are similar in other ways besides being highly sociable and living in the same geographic areas. The capacity to develop dominant and subordinate relationships; the need for companionship; the motivation for imitation and bullying —

11

are all mutual behavior patterns for man and wolf. It can almost be said that man and wolf were predestined to live together in a new social state awaiting only the gradual accumulations of fleeting contacts that would grow into permanent bonds. The form of the evolving relationships from wild wolf to trained pet, to domesticated dog, that took place over thousands of years can only be surmised, but surely it had its basis in benefits that flowed both to man and wolf.

Coming Together

A dog so often seen sitting or lying quietly at the feet of its owner is the end product of selective breeding that has taken place over probably at least thirty thousand years. Such a time span would permit over ten thousand generations of dogs, reproducing at an average age of about three years. Their breeding would be managed, intentionally or otherwise, by about half as many owners. Starting with the result of randomly selective matings of the original wolf population, native people, probably of mid-Asia, at the end of the Middle Paleolithic period began the process of forced or controlled matings. We will never be certain about the early coming together of man and the native wolf, but the remains of domestic dogs in the villages and campsites of the later Mesolithic people of Eastern Europe, Asia, and North America are solid evidence of the gradual process of selective breeding.

But what forces caused the earliest merging of man and wolf? The constant need for food could move them to watch and follow as one or the other managed to kill some quarry for the day's meal while the other went hungry. Squatting at a distance, hidden and fearful, and later gradually slinking closer to eye the tearing of the dead carcass, the hungry ones would be emboldened finally to test the tolerance of the other and hope to usurp the carcass. The slightest snarl, of course, would send all intruders scurrying, whether man or dog, to a safe distance where the cycle of desire that leads to action would begin again. No doubt the scene was repeated many times at many places before sufficient confidence prevailed and an uneasy acceptance resulted in the first tentative unions.

We know that these unions must have been caused by a profound need. A group of primitive people slashing and hacking with stone tools at the remains of a mastodon and hastily gorging on chunks and strips of bloody meat would surely bring forth the wolves drawn by the stench of the disemboweled carcass. Alternatively, a large wild animal might have been brought to bay by wolves as it tried to defend itself against these small aggressors. The tribal band, hearing the howls and grunts from the raging contest, would be drawn instinctively to the scene. Once down,

12

the wild animal would be torn apart by the slashing teeth of the pack. Now it would be man's turn to become the aggressor as he saw the valuable spoil and drove off the marauding band to claim the prize. Soon it would grow dark and the tribal band would be sitting around the campfire. Suddenly the leader of the group, seeing the wolves' bright eyes reflected in the firelight, would tear out a rib bone from the dead hulk and throw it to the watchful bank of scavengers. The crunch of bone soon heard from the shadows would be the first sound of communication that would lead eventually to a new level of understanding and mutual acceptance between these two who heretofore were competitors. The first time the wolf was fed by man began the long process of domestication. From this chance happening, the growth and development of productive relationships and achievements began. This bond of acceptance was a crucial step in man's future path and, of course, the subsequent breeding of the domesticated dog.

Once started, the possibilities were many for semi-wild canines to serve as aides to man. For how long the mere role of scavenger was played cannot be told, but certainly the running together of man and semi-wild wolves would become ever closer as mutual dependence developed. Traveling in bands, as they moved from hunting ground to hunting ground in their constant search for food, the groups of Paleolithic hunters and their wild canine companions were no doubt soon melded into an easy relationship. Many years and generations must have elapsed between the first act of communication, the throwing of a useless bone or piece of entrail to the wild wolf, and the more accepted status of a tolerated companion dutifully cleaning up campsite debris to gain food left by primitive man.

Intelligent animals such as canids do not develop an entirely new behavior through a sudden experience. Change occurs only by the slow association of responses to many recurrences of the same type of event. While the urge to satisfy hunger is strong, it was no doubt overcome in semi-wild wolves when the biological forces of nature drove them to acts of reproduction. The eventual withdrawal of the bitches to secluded holes for birthing and their later return with shy and skittery offspring, would soon result in man recognizing this new possibility for an orderly gain in canine numbers. He would find the situation similar in many ways to the important events within his own family group that resulted in the addition of children. Not only children appeared from time to time eventually to add strength of numbers to the wandering band, but also the bounty of small canines. What excitement the puppies must have created at first as a focus of interest and wonder.

Gradually, such arrivals must have caused a shift in attitude. Puppies would be accepted casually by the adults of the band and left to charm and entertain the young members. A new role for these canids emerged, that of plaything for the young to be enjoyed during leisure times. When all were full and relaxed after feasting on a new kill, the wild canine puppies, less fearful than either their mother or the wiser older canines that still held man with an uneasy regard, crept closer to the offered hand of the small child to smell and, hopefully, taste a bit of food.

A smell, a lick, a bite of food, and a dash away was probably repeated many, many times before there was a touch on the canine coat by the small hand. It most likely was a Paleo-Indian child who became the first human to have a pet of a wild dog and to take it along the second great step toward domestication.

Scavenging companion to the tribe and plaything for the young were, no doubt, the first roles for these partially tamed pets. Playful when young, skittish and nipping as they grew, and snarly and bold as adults, they were little different in general appearance and manner of survival from the wild wolf population. Of special importance was the fact that they willingly shared the same territory with another friendly tribal band, the humans.

The attacks on wild beasts that roamed the area continued as before. Unbeknown to these wild dogs, the act of hunting would soon be the other vital half of a working relationship that was to develop with the hunters of the tribe. The natural urges to satisfy hunger and to protect themselves would drive them to trail game and give chase to camp intruders. Their pursuit of quarry was the signal for man to follow and keep in sight this new leader of the hunt.

Here, for the first time, the order was set in which man and dog pursue game to this day: first the dog and then the man. The wild pet was swifter and better suited to smell the scent and see the spoor left by the wild beast. These traits, soon noticed by the hardy leader of the tribe, would be judged to be of great worth by lending an added measure of security to the tribal existence that depended so heavily on the success of the hunt. Bands of Paleo-Indians that learned to use these semi-wild canines in this role would have an advantage over those who lacked the knowledge and ability to form a team with these intelligent and wily animals. Favored also would be the tribe whose chief formed a special alliance with a strong and sagacious leader of a canine pack.

The ability to find game unseen by man may have caused wonder that led to the bearing of special gifts and reverence. A tribe with a pair of wise leaders would be fortunate indeed. A successful hunt deserved some

14

mark or ritual to ensure continued success. To the tribal chief would go a choice cut, and to the leader of the pack, the heart, liver, or entrails. These rewards would not be thrown rudely at the wildly howling canids that encircled the kill, but carefully handed as a special symbol from the chief hunter to his companion of the hunt, the canid pack leader. No longer just scavengers of the tribe, these ancestors of the dog would be equals, whose presence in the group provided new security from attack and far greater chance of survival because of help in the quest for food.

What was the relationship when the hunters failed? A sudden, harsh change in climate or the seasons could result in the migration of game from one region to another, or disease could strike and eliminate the favored quarry from the tribal territory. Once plentiful game tracked and killed with relative ease would disappear. Hungry people would question the skill and bravery of the leader and his canid aide. When the preferred game was no longer to be found, it perhaps was reasoned that it was a loss of special strength to trail and sense the presence of wild beasts which caused the tribe to suffer.

Food was needed! A new leader could help! The canid leader should be used as a sacrifice to change the weather or cause the game to reappear! Cries, interspersed with vain efforts to find food, would rack the tribal band along the way to starvation and death. The leader vainly trying to fulfill his role to the end while protecting his noble aide and companion on the hunt would, at last, succumb to the needs of the tribe and kill, one by one, the lesser members of the hunting pack. Each, in turn, would serve man in a new role, as food in time of shortage.

When an excess number were again in the pack, they might serve as special fare to supplement the other beasts slaughtered at the tribal board. The wisest of leaders, by experience, would be aware of periodic famines. He would see the repeated actions of the bitch canines and the later return with many wild little ones, which, when food was plentiful, would grow within a season to a size that could help in the hunt, and less desirable dogs could be killed to feed the band when food was scarce. This newest role for the wild canine would prove to be the most important for many thousands of years. It would ensure survival of the tribe and result in culling and selective breeding as the lesser prized members of the canid band were slaughtered.

Paleolithic man of the Upper Pleistocene Era, about ten thousand to thirty thousand years ago, was living in the last ice age. Those peoples, on the march for food and living near the massive glaciers of the northern hemisphere, constructed huts from poles and mammoth rib bones covered with animal skins. The huts had floors that were scooped out of the soil as a protection against drafts and were warmed by hearths located both inside and outside. The hut coverings and clothes were made from the skins of the deer and bison.

Survival in this harsh period, even as now, was dependent on food, shelter, and warmth. A tender morsel of meat, a sheltered place close to the fire, and a piece of skin covered with a soft fur pile would be prized. Light textured fur from the underbelly of the larger animals or from the swift smaller beasts could be used to decorate the special cloak of the chief or to wrap the newborn infant. Tamed canid pets, descended from the wolf that roamed the tribal campground between hunts, surely would be seen as a source of fine covering if skin was removed and cured when the fur was full and deep.

The canids' important role as aide to the chief gave protection from destruction until a time when sparse hunting drove the chief to slaughter the less favored of his pack. Not only could the meat of the dogs be eaten, their skin could make a fine cover. Additionally, the pelt could have a special significance since it was once the holder of a body with skills of the hunt. It would be deemed better than all others to convey the powers needed to survive.

As ages passed, the ancestral dog served man as a guard against wild beasts and tribal foes, as a source of food and clothing, and as a hunter. Slowly, man developed greater power and skill in the chase as his weapons became more sophisticated. This allowed him to assert mastery over the tamed canid hunters by controlling their response to the movements of the quarry and eventually directing complex actions to achieve greater hunting success.

This gradual change over centuries, from wild wolf hunter to partner in the chase and finally to trained tool of the hunter chieftain, ultimately forced the canid into a subservient role. No longer an equal or treated as one with special powers, the trained pets of the tribe now would fill increasingly mundane roles. The time would come when their presence during the hunt would be considered disadvantageous or worthless for certain quarry. Game, too swift for dogs, such as the deer or lynx, would be frightened by the chase of the dog beyond the range of the following hunter group. Smaller animals, holed by dogs and thus out of reach of the men armed with clubs and lances, would be lost.

Now often a nuisance to the hunter, the pack would remain at camp, lounging and stealing food when free of kicks and rebukes from the women and children. Although often still playthings, they would be molested by the children who played at hunting with the dogs as game. The larger ones would serve yet another role, as an animal to mount and ride. Young legs spread wide, hands clutching the neck fur to hold the rider in place, the Paleo-Indian children would dominate their pets. The women of the tribe would see this carrier of children in a new light. The heavy load of sticks and branches gathered in a distant wood could be loaded onto the backs of the larger dogs. Those trained to the chase would now be trained as pack animals to aid the women in gathering wood for the hearths. Later, when the movable poles that held the skins for the huts came down and the people were ready for migration to a warmer region or a more bountiful hunting area, the once proud hunting pack would be harnessed to the poles as beasts of burden and goaded to troop along with the possessions of the tribe.

Although they filled a lowly role as the first beasts of burden of the Paleo-Indians, some trained pets would regain in future years a measure of their former dash and freedom while dragging at high speed a sled of poles across the frozen snow and ice of the glacial steppes and frigid North. The invention of the hitch by some clever Paleolithic member of a traveling band, so that two or more dogs could drag a load of meat, skins, and furs lashed between two longer poles, was a great step toward man's brighter future. Once again, the dog would be both the catalyst and provider that permitted a significant advance toward civilization for man.

The trained pets of the wandering bands now served many uses— scavenger, hunter, plaything, load bearer, companion, and source of food and clothing. Even in the role of companion there were special benefits. The normal body temperature of the canid at 105° Farenheit, compared to the normal temperature of the human at 98.6°, would offer a source of heat. Under the trying circumstances of frigid weather, Paleo-Indians with canid pets could have extra warmth by huddling together against the cold. Children sleeping with puppies could survive the coldest night, while the aged hunter, bedded down with his old companion of the trail, could pass the winter in relative comfort. Finally, the warrior, laid down in death with his dog, was judged to have warmth and companionship during this longest of all nights.

Man's Best Friend

While the course toward full transformation of the wolf into the dog can only be conjectured, there is little doubt that a full state of domestication was achieved over the twenty thousand year period prior to the start of the Mesolithic Era. The training and breeding of dogs was an ancient art; modern breeders have added little except greater specialization. All the main groups of dogs were created by these

Mesolithic folk long before there was a written record of the accomplishment. The extraordinary variability that is evident in this canid species was deliberately sought by early man. Minor differences emerged that suited the needs of the breeder and were carefully reproduced again and again to fix the new features. Dogs pass quickly through many generations, thus permitting the rapid selection of special characteristics. Breeding for large or small size, curly or straight hair, a change in the color of the coat, even a change in the shape of the ears, might be accomplished within the life of an individual breeder.

During the Mesolithic period the chance encounters of relatively isolated human groups and their dogs also led to changes in the dog populations. There is ample evidence that by the post-glacial period, groups of people were making contact with other groups. The genetic crosses that these meetings made possible were precisely what was needed to add variety to the dog populations. During trading, war, or friendly gatherings, there were opportunities for matings of dogs from one tribal band with the dogs from afar. While tribes with neighboring territories probably had dog breeds that were quite similar, across large land areas such as the Asian, North American, or European Continents, there would have been significant differences.

Breeding for size, shape, and speed for the hunt would have been the primary focus of the early Mesolithic hunters. The agricultural revolution was a major factor in dog breeding as new roles were identified for this first domesticated animal. A good dog for the hunter in the forest would not be suited for herding semidomesticated stock or keeping rodents at bay in graneries. Man's previous accomplishments at breeding brought forth dogs tamed and trained to hunt, to guard, and to scavenge. Now new sizes and types of dogs were needed. There would have to be greater selective breeding and for specific purposes. It was an extraordinary age when man subjected wild creatures and plants to his selective whim. Various new breeds of dogs accompanied the wandering groups during their far-ranging movements that were now possible by the carrying of edible grain and the breeding of stock for meat and milk while along the route. There was wide-scale intermixing of both people and dogs. Interbreeding of dogs was common and varieties proliferated. Recognizably different breeds of dogs have been uncovered from ancient campsites of that time. By five thousand years ago, there were at least five major identifiable kinds—hunters, herders, guards, workers, and toys. Evolving from a species in direct competition with man to a species unmatched by any other living creature, the dog, by the end of the Mesolithic Era, truly had become man's best aide and friend.

18

A graphic representation of the transformation of a wild wolf population into the variety of types of modern dogs is shown on page 6. It has been suggested that the primary ancestor of North American dogs is the Chinese wolf, *Canis lupus chanco*. It has been suggested also that European and western Asian dogs may have evolved from small races of the Middle East wolf. At some unknown time and place in central Asia, began man's long relationship with the dog.

Archeological evidence from sites in Asia and North America suggests that by the end of the Middle Paleolithic Age the process of random selection had probably resulted in the first wild pets. The association of small wolves and man probably occurred at many times and many places in eastern Asia until it was not uncommon to have tamed wolf/dogs as a Paleo-Indian family possession. Over a twenty thousand year period, the slow but certain domestication of the dog ensued until by the beginning of the Mesolithic culture the true dog was a common companion of man.

While the illustration covers an approximate thirty thousand year period, it was in the latter part of this time-span that the intermixing of types occurred that has resulted in the great number of modern breeds. During the early ages and into the present, man consciously expanded the breeding of dog with dog and now and then with differing varieties of wolves, to produce by planned selection ever more varied species. At times, because of abandonment or loss as the tribal band moved on or was annihilated, the once prized possession was left to itself or to associate with its wild cousins. On these occasions, processes of planned and specific selection were abruptly ended, and soon random matings produced the feral dogs that even today roam the world.

Because of the vast number of individual decisions by man that were brought to bear on the selective breeding of the dog and because of the numerous chance happenings that broke or altered the developing trends, there is today a vast population of at least eight hundred distinctly different true-breeding types throughout the world. Additionally, worldwide there is a large group of physically similar feral dogs. Alas, the ancestor of them all, the poor wolf, has been chased and hunted by modern man so that there are but a few remaining races, and, in most countries, the wolf is fast becoming an endangered species.

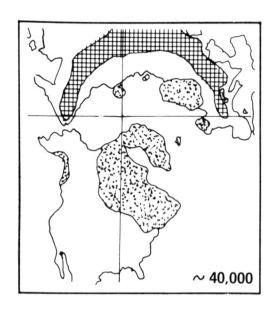

ICE EXTENSION

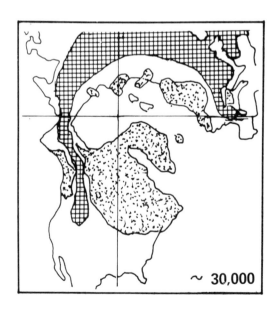

OCCUPIED AREAS

Ice extension and archeological complex areas over Eurasia and North America at about 40,000 and 30,000 years ago. (After Muller-Beck, 1966.)

The Historical Record

At various places during the Upper Paleolithic Era man had contacts with wolves. The wolf *Canis lupus* includes a large number of varieties indicated by subspecific names such as *Canis lupus pallipes*, which ranges from the plains south of the Himalayas in India to as far west as Syria and Israel; *Canis lupus battai* and *Canis lupus bodopoilax*, once found in Japan; and *Canis lupus chanco*, whose home is today in China, Manchuria, Mongolia, Tibet, and southwest Russia. All these varieties and some other species of wild canids can be bred with domesticated dogs.

It is recorded frequently in early histories that the American Indians and Eskimos caused forced breeding of their bitches when in heat by tying them out at night when wolves were in the area. This practice to improve the native stock was at times successful and reintroduced wolf genes into the strain of dog being raised by the local people. It certainly was possible that this method of breeding caused variations in temperament, size, and length and color of coat as significant as the differences that existed among the wild canids. It also is possible that the North American coyote, the South American fox, the Eurasian jackal, and the African jackal and hunting dog contributed genes to the early dog population in those respective areas.

During the Upper Paleolithic Era, which lasted through the final glacial period, man had adapted to harsh circumstances and provided himself the basic necessities of life. It was during this glacial period, between ten thousand and thirty thousand years ago, that the different races of modern man emerged, resulting in the skin color, hair, and physical characteristics that still differentiate the races today. Ice fields spread across Europe, Asia, and North America. In what is now the United States, the ice sheets of the Wisconsin Glacial Era spread as far south as New York and the Great Plains. The mountainous, western third of the continent was covered with an ice mass as far south as Washington. It was during this period, when sea levels were lowered because of the vast amount of water that was locked in the glacial ice, that *Homo sapiens* crossed into the continents of Australia and North America. The lowering of sea levels exposed new lands that connected Asia with North America across the Bering Strait region. Man's passage

21

across these new lands would have been relatively easy; he merely followed the wild game as it spread slowly over the newly vegetated terrain.

Man's passage to Australia was by way of the Indonesian archipelago and probably accompanying him was the semi-domesticated form of the Chinese wolf. This dog later became feral and is now known as the Dingo. The Chinese wolf is smaller and slighter than the North American wolf and has a shorter coat with little undercoat. It is surprisingly fast and has great endurance. Although it is larger, its slenderness and general appearance are similar to those of the Dingo. The Australian Dingo still retains some characteristics that are associated with domestication: it has white markings on the fur, a wide muzzle, and an expanded nose. Whether the original stock taken to Australia was semi-domesticated or fully domesticated will never be known. Whatever the pattern, by modern times, the first European settlers in Australia were greeted by canids that looked like wolves but exhibited many dog-like manners and features. Because of its history, the Dingo is considered by many anthropologists to be an approximation or prototype of the earliest dogs.

In another direction out of the Eurasian heartland went Paleo-Indians who finally entered the North American Continent by way of Alaska. There is little doubt that these men and women brought along primitive dogs from somewhere in northeast Asia. While there has been a great amount of archeological work done in the past fifty years that has shed light on the history of man's crossing the Bering Strait, the skeletal remains of neither these early people nor their dogs have as yet been positively identified in North America. To date, the presence of these early inhabitants has been confirmed only by association with mammoth kills and the stone points embedded in the skeletal remains of these great beasts.

The origins and diffusion of the American Paleo-Indians has been a gradually evolving story as the archeological evidence has mounted. The comprehensive picture presented by Dr. Hansjurgen Muller-Beck in 1966 is today judged as most logical. Based on an extensive study of the tools of the European, Asian, and American Paleolithic people and the topographical isolation of North America caused by the advancing ice sheets of the Wisconsin Glacial period, Muller-Beck shows the existence of two distinct diffusions of people; the first occurred between thirty thousand and twenty-six thousand years ago, and the second about twelve thousand to ten thousand years ago. These advances and the attendant ice barriers are indicated on the maps on pages 20 and 23,

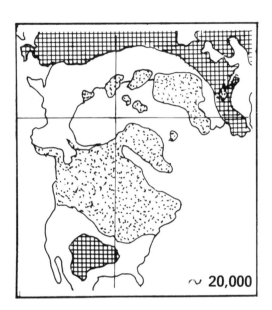

~ 20,000

ICE EXTENSION

OCCUPIED AREAS

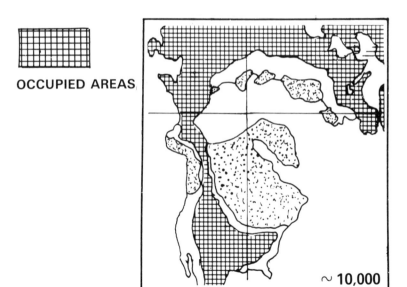

~ 10,000

Ice extension and archeological complex areas over Eurasia and North America at about 20,000 and 10,000 years ago. (After Muller-Beck, 1966.)

23

where conditions at ten thousand year intervals are shown. From forty thousand to thirty thousand years ago (page 20), there occurred a gradual diffusion of people that used specialized projectile points as hunters of the open plains that stretched across the Eurasian landmass to the Bering Sea. Between thirty thousand and ten thousand years ago, a dry land bridge existed between Asia and America when the sea level fell about one hundred twenty-five feet (forty meters) below the present level. The land bridge reached its maximum width about twenty thousand years ago. The shallowest part of the now-submerged region between Siberia and Alaska is about one hundred ten to one hundred twenty-five feet below the sea. During the existence of this land bridge, it would have been easy for man and dog to cross into North America, then a continuous land mass with Asia. Over this land bridge (page 20) spread the woolly mammoth, caribou, and other animals, followed by man. The illustration on page 23 shows conditions about twenty thousand years ago when a large ice barrier south of Alaska was formed through contact between the Cordilleran and Laurentide ice sheets. This barrier lasted with variations in size during a period from about twenty-three thousand to thirteen thousand years ago and completely sealed southern North America from migration. After the glacial ice receded (page 23), contact with earlier migrants into North America would have been possible.

Of course, for hundreds of years, only people that had adapted, in Asia, to the cold conditions to be encountered when living near the ice barrier could have survived the grueling journey east and south from Asia and Alaska. By twelve thousand years ago, they surely entered America and spread across the open land to the south in expanding number. This new wave of hunters, equipped with well-formed projectile points and accompanied by the dog, moved at a steady rate to reach the tip of South America by ten thousand five hundred years ago.

Therefore, as permitted by the topographical and glacial features that existed during the last forty thousand years, the invasion of man into the New World during the last ice age could have occurred about thirty thousand to twenty-six thousand years ago. Unfortunately, there is documented archeological evidence of his stay at only a few sites. Included are two in Mexico, dated about twenty-two thousand B.P., where a resharpened quartz and obsidian scraper were found with mastodon bones; two in Colorado dated about twenty thousand B.P., where the cracked bones of mammoths, camels, horses, and bison mark an early kill site; and one at Old Crow Basin in the northern Yukon, where artifacts tested by the carbon-14 method show an age of about thirty thousand years. The Old Crow sites have produced well-formed tools of bone, cracked and butchered bones of many different types of animals, and the jaws of several domesticated dogs, some of which appear on the basis of color staining to be at least thirty thousand years old. This latter find is of special significance since it may be about twenty thousand years older than the Jaguar Cave dogs found in Idaho.

The Old Crow sites, under study by teams of archeologists, paleontologists, and geologists from the University of Toronto, the National Museum of Canada, and the University of Alberta are yielding new evidence that these early Paleo-Indians crossed the land bridge from Asia. A people expert in working bone occupied periodically the three thousand square mile Old Crow Basin with numerous Ice Age wild game animals. Over thousands of years, the skeletal remains of their butchering have been preserved beneath layers of sediment that is now being washed away at bends in the Old Crow River. Subsequently cleaned, classified, and studied, they reveal to paleontologists, such as Dr. Brenda F. Beebe of the University of Toronto, clues about the animal population, the ecosystem, and the life style of these early people in North America. The Old Crow dogs of greatest age occur in two size ranges—one small (Terrier size) and the other large (Eskimo Dog size).

Also at the archeological site of Trail Creek, Alaska, on the Seward Peninsula, teeth of small dogs have been recovered that apparently date to about 13,000 B.P. About the domesticated dog remains at Old Crow, Dr. Beebe states that "another mandible of particular interest is much more heavily mineralized, resembling bone dated to ca. 30,000 B.P. The specimen exhibits characters seen in the early states of dog domestication: (1) the teeth remain wolf-sized, and (2) the jaw is heavy and shortened causing overlap in the premolar dental series. If future dating of this specimen should confirm the ca. 30,000 B.P. date, it would suggest that dogs were domesticated from wolves at a much earlier time in prehistory than commonly believed."

This Old Crow dog, because of its probable age, is farthest back in the development of the domesticated dog. Because of jaw shape and location and orientation of the teeth, it is possible for Dr. Beebe to distinguish this specimen as an animal of wolf ancestory that is in the early stages of domestication. Let us hope that during future studies of Old Crow skeletal remains, other specimens of wolf/dog will be uncovered so that confirming carbon-14 evidence will be obtained.

Just as the Wisconsin Ice Age closed the route to the interior of North America, so the knowledge about man's presence is seemingly closed for the ten thousand year period following these earliest finds. Few archeological sites have been discovered in North and South America that are dated between about twenty thousand and about twelve thousand years ago. It is as if darkness enveloped the New World to end its new habitation by people from Asia. One can only speculate about the true course of events that left such a void in the evidence of man's presence south of the great ice sheets that blocked passage from the north during this long interval of time.

Disease of the dimensions of a plague, ignorance in the ways of survival under climatological change, or extermination by animal predators could all have played a part in the radical reduction or total elimination of these earliest of Paleo-Indians so that their living sites are too limited to be chanced upon. Possibly, some evidence will emerge with time, but until then, the story of man's presence in America and the history of the dog in the New World must begin anew with the record of the first population explosion caused by the second invasion of man into interior America. Firm evidence exists at numerous kill sites that men, women, and children burst upon the land through the ice-free corridor about twelve thousand years ago. The first evidence was provided by the now famous site at Clovis, New Mexico.

The first of these finds produced the now famous Clovis fluted point that is used to link discoveries of similar age and culture. In the Southern High Plains, adjacent to the Rocky Mountain foothills and desert basin area of the southwest, Clovis points have been associated with the skeletons of elephant, mastodon, bison, horse, and other late glacial period mammals, as well as the previously noted mammoth of this period. Hearth charcoal from certain sites has been used to date the time of the "kill" by carbon-14 dating, giving an age of eleven thousand to twelve thousand years.

Additionally, it is known that a small band of these primitive hunters occupied a cave in Idaho during the same period and left in their rubbish the bones of a domesticated dog. Surprisingly, there was not just one size of dog, but two—a small terrier type and a larger wolf-like or Eskimo Dog. This find of semi-domesticated dog skeletal remains is the earliest south of the Arctic region. The similar ages for the ancient *Canis famil-iaris* in the Near East and America leads to the view that the origin of all dogs will be found somewhere between these two areas—in western China or Tibet.

Recent work by anthropologists Stanley J. Olsen and John W. Olsen suggests that the Chinese or Tibetan wolf (*Canis lupus chanco*) is the most likely ancestor of the dogs that accompanied early man. This is not to deny that large northern wolves and coyotes may have been bred to dogs that greeted the first explorers many thousands of years later.

As can be seen from the descriptions of skeletal finds, zoologists typically have very little osteological material to study in forming judgments or conclusions. Complete skulls or jaw bones are rare, and usually, fragments of jaws and some teeth or bones are all that is available. Particular care must be exercised in establishing criteria for identification, and small differences in structure of the osteological remains must be painstakingly sought for detailed analysis. Nevertheless, morphological characteristics are sufficient to make distinctions even if the reasons for differences between wild and domestic *Canis* are not fully understood.

The recent studies by Olsen and Olsen have focused attention on a particular characteristic of the domestic dog that appears consistently through the past and, therefore, can be considered for identification purposes. The illustration on page 28 originally appeared in *Science,* as part of the paper "The Chinese Wolf, Ancestor of New World Dogs." The lower jaw bones (mandibles) are from eight different American dogs spanning more than ten thousand years and one from China that is seven thousand years old. All show the characteristic "turned-back" top of the vertical side of the portion of the jaw that moves against the skull. This portion of the mandible has muscle attached for closing the jaw.

The amount of overhang seemingly is related to the diet of the animal. Those with a varied diet that includes foods in addition to meat have this feature on the jawbone. Those that are strictly carnivorous, such as wolves, cats, and badgers, have no overhang but rather a jawbone with symmetrically rounded crests. Interestingly, one wolf has the overhang as a feature of the jawbone and it is the Chinese wolf, *Canis lupus chanco.* The striking difference in this portion of the jaw of this wolf and those of the North American wolf, coyote, and jackal is shown on page 30. This clear evidence of a diagnostic trait in the jaws of all dogs and only one subspecies of wolf certainly links them uniquely. It is almost certain that this new method of identification will be used increasingly to remove the last doubt about the origin of the dogs that first entered North America, and also to confirm the ancestry of all dogs.

Dog, Wolf, or Coyote?

While the shape of the ascending portion of the lower jawbone is a critical indicator of that descendant of wolf called *Canis familiaris*, there unfortunately are many archeological finds that do not contain this portion of the jaw. Some contain just the heavy middle section of the lower jaw, with or without teeth. Others contain pieces of the skull and a few of the major leg bones. In some few excavations, archeologists find a

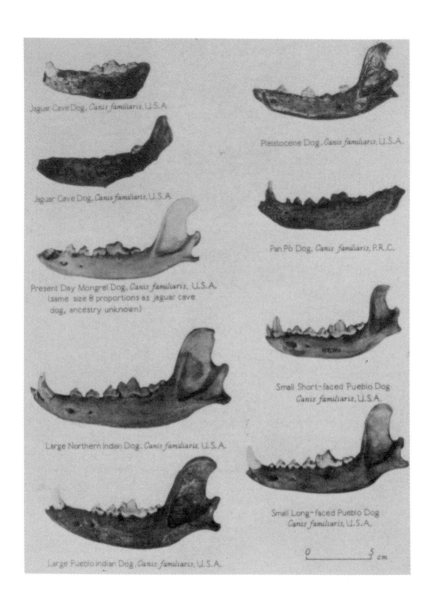

Lower jawbones of American and Chinese dogs. (Olsen and Olsen, 1977.)

complete skeleton and in others the remains of a dog buried with care beside a child or adult. No matter how slight or complete the remains in the excavation, it is the task of the paleontologists and/or anthropologists to study the remains and to consider the features of the skeleton in order to identify the species. Except for a few examples of mummified dogs, the dog remains found in archeological sites are skeletal and in most excavations only skulls and jaws have been collected. Hence, research on features of the osteological remains has focused on skull traits that can be used to determine whether they are of dog, wolf, or coyote.

Definitive studies by William G. Haag in 1948 and by Barbara Lawrence and William H. Bossert in 1967 serve as the basis for current decisions about the remains of *Canis* species under archeological study. Haag's work established a measuring system that is based on the skulls of eight types of ancient and recent dogs. Measurements of representative samples of dog skulls from southeastern shell heap middens, northwest and Aleutian sites, and Siberia and Alaska serve as the basis for his conclusions about the origin and domestication of the dog. The dog skeletons studied by Haag were from widely different cultures and from prehistoric to current occupations of North America. In most instances the dog bones are from a number of similar sites rather than a single site, to give an accurate representation of the range of measurements.

To provide a further basis for identification, Lawrence and Bossert use many of the means of measurements set by Haag in their multiple character analysis of a broadly representative sample of the skulls of wolf, coyote, and dog. Prior to this work, the identification of skulls of the members of the genus *Canis* was imprecise at best, and completely unfounded in some cases. The clear identity of a find is of considerable importance to archeological researchers, and is important also to students of ethnology and even anthropology. For example, evidence of fossil animals can contribute to a fuller understanding of the time level of certain ancient sites and of the ecosystem of the inhabitants. Lawrence and Bossert show that combinations of characters separate wolf, coyote, and dog, even when size is eliminated as a character. Using these indicators, it is usually possible to establish whether skeletal remains, however ancient, are of dog, wolf, or coyote.

In the Lawrence and Bossert study, test populations of each species consist of adult animals of both sexes selected randomly. For the wolves, *Canis lupus,* the group includes only North American races. For coyotes, *Canis latrans,* specimens were chosen from a wide geographic area of the original range of the species. For dogs, *Canis familiaris,* the selection is of many wolf-like and coyote-like specimens.

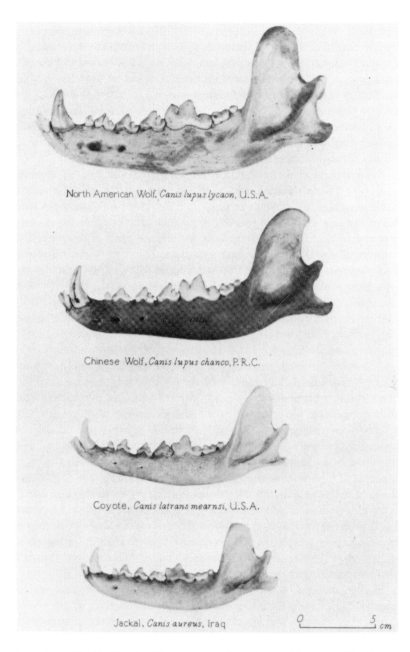

North American Wolf, *Canis lupus lycaon*, U.S.A.

Chinese Wolf, *Canis lupus chanco*, P.R.C.

Coyote, *Canis latrans mearnsi*, U.S.A.

Jackal, *Canis aureus*, Iraq

0 —————— 5 cm

Lower jaws of Canids. Note the right-turning portion at the top of the ramus of the Chinese wolf, attributed to be the possible ancestor of the domestic dog. (Olsen and Olsen, 1977.)

Since the goal of the study is to identify measurements that are most different among the three species, a larger number of characteristics are included. Forty-two different measurements form the initial group. These are reduced by regression analysis to twenty-four that serve as the final test group. Thirteen concern skull shape and eleven relate to tooth form.

So that the results can be used to identify a wolf, coyote, or dog, whether large or small, the effect of size is eliminated as a factor by relating all measurements to total length of skull. The results of each measurement are compared against similar results for each species. From the analysis, features of diagnostic value for dog, wolf, and coyote are found, although it is shown that no single feature occurs without overlap between a pair of species. The basic skull length measurement plus nine cranial and six tooth measurements are critical for identification. Of these characters, thirteen involve the skull and two the lower jaw.

Wolves and coyotes are found to differ most in the relative development of the rostrum and of the brain-case. Wolves have a relatively large jaw and small head. The former is probably due to the larger size animals that are its source of food. The heavy maxilla (see page 32), large teeth, and width of jaw all support the formation of a powerful jaw. These features combined with massiveness of the zygomatic arch contribute to the great crushing action of the jaws.

Coyotes, eaters of small animals, have a rather large head and small jaw with small, narrow teeth. Because the zygomatic arch is less massive, the skull is long and slender in appearance when compared to a wolf skull.

Since dogs are essentially small wolves, they can be distinguished from coyotes by many of the proportions of muzzle and head. Unfortunately, since they exhibit great variability, no single set of characters can be used to identify this species clearly. In fact, because the dog lacks homogeneity, a particular skull might resemble superficially either wolf or coyote rather than dog. This means that some care must be exercised in calling the remains dog and that the identification characters depend on whether the skull is wolf-like or coyote-like in general appearance.

Highly modified or developed breeds of dogs are fairly easily identified by the disproportionate size of the head. Others are identified by the rather large frontal sinuses and steep angle of the forehead. Some show a well-developed "stop" as the rostrum and brain-case meet at more of an angle than is usual in wild canids. Less modified breeds, including many mongrels, differ from wolves in having relatively small teeth and an elongated palate so that the back is well rear of the second molars. The greater size of the canine teeth in dogs reflects their relationship to

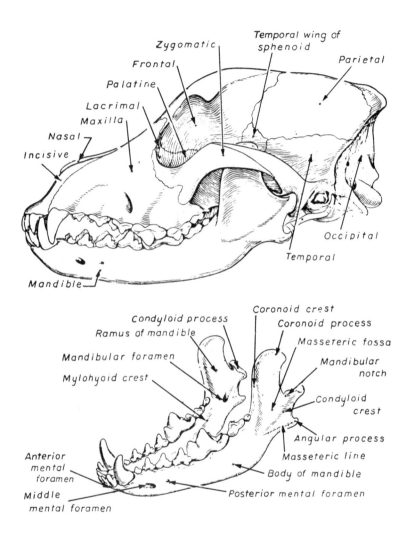

Features of the skull and mandible of the dog that are useful in the identification of skeletal remains from archeological sites. (From Miller, 1964.)

wolves, and dogs have a greater width across the incisors. Alternatively, the last upper molar in the dog is relatively small when compared to both the wolf and coyote and is therefore a particularly good distinguishing feature. This size apparently results from the long period of domestication.

Tests of skeletal remains of skull and mandible based on the Lawrence and Bossert characters show that all three species are sharply distinct, but that wolves and dogs resemble each other more than either resembles the coyote. The use of measurements such as these, to the greatest extent possible, of the archeological finds at ancient sites has permitted full development of the record of dogs and the association with man since Paleolithic times.

Dating the Find

How old are these bones? The accurate answer to this question has troubled the mind of many an archeologist since the beginning of serious research into the prehistory of man. The science of geology offered a first approach to an answer. The archeologists, faced with the task of building up an account of the past on the basis of bones and artifacts uncovered in the excavations, used the geologic evidence to advantage. Geologists, in ordering their discoveries, used the principle of successive layering to set the order of events that caused varying deposits of earth and rock. Along with the record of the characteristic remains of plants and animals within the layers, a succession of geological periods or epochs is evident and may be traceable over extended areas.

Archeologists, realizing that the layers of deposition at archeological sites can be studied in the same manner, excavate by observing coherent sequences of occupation zones that are found in the successive layers. This stratigraphic method remains today the essential basis for archeological studies and permits the finds to be set in chronological order. The method provides the essential for effective dating, gives an accurate sequence, and provides a relative chronology. Layer A can be shown to lie over layer B, which in turn is over layer C, and each has its own thickness; but unfortunately, only relative age is known. The precise age or duration of the zones can only be guessed by this process.

During the 1800s, with the increasing numbers of studies and increasing numbers of artifacts accumulating in the museums, a second conceptual tool was advanced to become the basic method by which curators and antiquarians set their collections in order. Divisions in prehistory relating to the artifacts of stone, bronze, and iron were recognized. This theoretical notion was confirmed about one hundred years ago by J. J. A. Worsaae, Keeper of Antiquities of the National Museum in Copenhagen, through his studies of the placement of objects of stone and bronze in stratigraphic layers at archeological sites. Although a somewhat crude scale in the measuring of time, the sequences of Paleolithic (old stone), Mesolithic (middle stone), Neolithic (new stone), bronze and iron ages are still used in Europe as convenient indicators.

Over the years some progress was made even in obtaining general agreement about the approximate number in thousands of years that these ages represented. Toward this end, the rate of deposit of sediments at the bottom of lakes and rivers, the successive layers of sediment from the melted water of glaciers, and the calculation of the climatic effects on earth due to small changes in its orbit around the sun were the methods available for setting absolute time. Even the work of the Egyptologists was brought to bear on this problem of dating. Their studies of inscriptions, astronomical records, and historical documents permitted the setting of a calendar of events. Combined with the record from Mesopotamia, the date of 5100 B.P. set the limit of recorded history.

While these methods were helpful enough for the ages back to the Neolithic, the accuracy was not good. For older events, the margin of error grew to many thousands of years and the dating methods became essentially worthless. Then in 1949, the problem of dating archeological sites was solved by a radically new procedure. Dr. Willard F. Libby in New York announced the first dates determined by carbon-14 measurement. This revolutionary process was a great boon to archeology and is the basis today of far more accurate dates for artifacts than processes previously known. The method, the potential for dating prehistory accurately, caused an immediate sensation, and, in time, Libby won the Nobel Prize for Chemistry.

This new method of dating was possible because of recent developments in atomic physics. The earth is constantly being bombarded by small, sub-atomic particles possessing very high energy. This cosmic radiation from outside our solar system sets off a number of atomic reactions when it comes in contact with the earth's atmosphere. The reaction that is important to archeologists is one that results in the production of small quantities of radiocarbon, a rare variety of the very common element carbon, that behaves chemically in the same way. Of course, carbon is present in the atmosphere (largely as the gas carbon dioxide), and is a fundamental constituent of all living things, both plant and animal. Radiocarbon, or carbon-14, is a little heavier than ordinary carbon-12. It is called an isotope of carbon and is truly rare, there being only one atom in the earth's atmosphere for every million atoms of the common isotope carbon-12.

Carbon-14 also is radioactive in that a slow and constant rate of decay occurs as it gives off tiny electrons and changes to nitrogen. The radioactive decay takes place at a known rate in such a way that half of a given sample of radiocarbon disappears after a time of about 5,500 years. Thus this decay takes place slowly for the carbon-14 that is found everywhere in the sea and land, in living or dead plant and animal tissues.

Because the creation and decay processes of carbon-14 are in balance, the proportion in the atmosphere is neither increasing nor decreasing, but remains constant at a known level. Its proportion to carbon-12 is therefore also constant and both are picked up by living plants and animals. Libby's realization was that when a plant or animal dies, since it ceases to take up carbon, the decay rate of the internally contained radioactive carbon-14 can be a time clock for dating. The radiocarbon method measures the proportion of carbon-14 left in a sample, and thus determines the age. The initial proportion when living is the well-known constant amount. We can measure the proportion left in the sample and calculate how long the decay process has continued. This time is the same as the age of the object in question. Therefore, the archeologists must find suitable samples for radiocarbon dating.

The age of the object and, more than likely, the age of the layer that surrounds the object, can be determined with an accuracy of a few hundred years. Carbonized seeds are best, being almost pure carbon—and only about twenty grams are needed. Wood charcoal is good, but care must be taken in the assessment since it may have been quite old when burned and buried so that a deceptively old age would be indicated by the test. Since there is little carbon in bone, about three hundred grams of bone are needed and best results are obtained when only the extracted protein collagen is used.

For each test the sample is destroyed so that unless there is an excess of material, it is a serious matter to proceed with dating. The sample is first cleaned carefully to remove foreign material and, if necessary, treated to extract any contaminating chemicals. It is then processed further to extract the carbon and to convert it to a form in which its radioactivity can be measured. Sometimes it is burned in pure oxygen to create carbon dioxide, which is either used directly, or converted to the liquid acetylene. The measurements are made with great care, using highly sensitive instruments, since the amount of radiation to be measured is very small, even in samples of fairly recent origin. Background radiation, cosmic radiation that penetrates the earth's atmosphere and reaches the earth's surface, is usually more than fifteen times greater than that to be measured in the sample and causes a severe problem. Special shielding and elaborate arrangements of radiation counters can minimize the effect. But, even so, the final determination is a statistical value such as 4800 B.P. plus or minus one hundred years. This counting error, plus one hundred in this case, is the deviation in the measurement due to the continuous, fluctuating level of the background radiation that prevailed during successive measurements of radioactivity of the sample. It can never be eliminated and can lead to confusion in judging actual age.

Usually one standard deviation is given. In the example, it means that there is a 66 percent probability that the correct value lies within the limits specified (i.e., 4700 B.P. to 4900 B.P.). It has a 95 percent probability of being within two standard deviations (4500 B.P. to 5000 B.P.), a 99.5 percent probability of being within three standard deviations (4500 B.P. to 5100 B.P.) and a finite, but very small probability, of being even outside these last ages. Therefore, the artifact in this example could be anywhere from about 4450 to 5150 years old.

There are other factors that cause radiation dating to be less precise than desirable. These relate to the basic assumptions about the dating theory. The half life of carbon-14, an absolute constant, has been assigned differing values as the measuring techniques are improved. The latest is 5,730 plus or minus 30 years, and is 162 years longer than the original determination by Libby in 1949. The presence of undetected contamination can influence the measurements severely and lead to error. The lack of uniform worldwide distribution of carbon-14 is minor and does not seriously affect the results. The last consideration, constancy of the radiation with time, unfortunately, is now discredited. Libby assumed originally that the effects of cosmic radiation do not vary and that the proportion of radiocarbon to ordinary carbon-12 in the atmosphere remains constant through time. By determining the age of wood samples from tree-ring studies and subsequently performing carbon-14 dating on the precisely determined samples, the analyses show clearly that the concentration of carbon-14 has varied in the atmosphere throughout time, and therefore in all living things throughout time.

Dendrochronology, the method of tree-ring dating that uses the annual growth ring of trees as a determinant, has come to improve further the accuracy of dating. Hans E. Luers, in 1970, developed corrections for radiocarbon dates back 6,250 years by using the bristle-cone pine. The corrections begin for dates about 2000 years ago and grow increasingly, but in a variable manner, to as much as a 1000 year correction at 6000 years before the present.

There may, of course, in time be further evidence about the appropriateness of the basic assumptions for the carbon-14 dating method. No doubt these will be taken into account to refine further our ability to date accurately the archeological site or remains. Using corrected half-life measurements, it now is possible to date objects to about forty thousand years. For older samples, too little radioactivity is left for an accurate measurement.

In our discussion of the date of various finds of dog remains, the radiocarbon date is critical. To compile the dates for the prehistoric dogs, the average age provided in the original report is rounded to the nearest hundred years. Considering the current difficulties in precise age determination, it is reasonable to consider a typical deviation of two hundred years to apply to each age. Nevertheless, the age determination by the Libby method of carbon-14 dating and corrected by Luers' dendrochronology, gives a dramatic and accurate view of the age of prehistoric dogs in America.

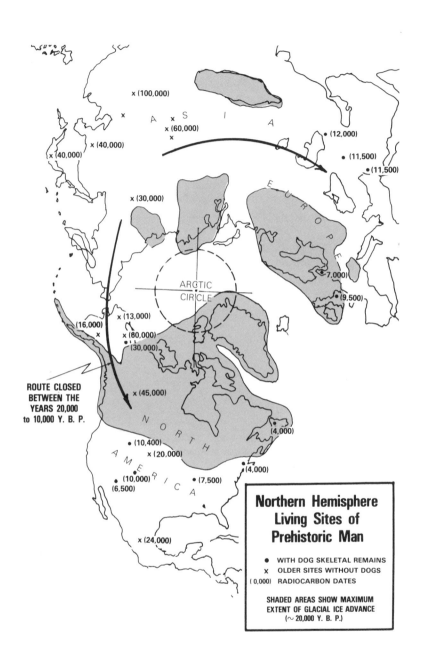

x (100,000)

x
x (60,000)
x

A S I A

x (40,000)

x (40,000)

x (40,000)

• (12,000)

• (11,500)

• (11,500)

x (30,000)

E U R O P E

• 7,000)

• (9,500)

ARCTIC
CIRCLE

x (13,000)

(16,000)
x

• (80,000)

(30,000)

N O R T H

x (45,000)

ROUTE CLOSED
BETWEEN THE
YEARS 20,000
to 10,000 Y. B. P.

• (4,000)

• (10,400)
x (20,000)

• (4,000)

A M E R I C A

• (10,000)   • (7,500)
(6,500)

x (24,000)

**Northern Hemisphere
Living Sites of
Prehistoric Man**

•   WITH DOG SKELETAL REMAINS
x   OLDER SITES WITHOUT DOGS
(0,000)   RADIOCARBON DATES

SHADED AREAS SHOW MAXIMUM
EXTENT OF GLACIAL ICE ADVANCE
(~ 20,000 Y. B. P.)

Old and New World Dogs

The techniques are now well established for dating the levels uncovered at archeological sites and for identifying the bones of dogs from the remains of animals found in the various levels. With each passing year, archeologists are discovering new sites that add to our understanding of the sequence of events that comprise the story of early man and his dog. Additionally, the bones and artifacts uncovered at older sites are analyzed anew for type of fauna and age. These old and new finds serve as the basis for a rapidly emerging chronology.

How rapid has been the addition of knowledge is shown by the fact that only twenty years ago it was accepted by all experts in the field of prehistory that the dog was domesticated only a few thousand years ago. Bones at living sites in Denmark and Germany placed the dog there about 5000 B.P. Dog remains uncovered at the village sites of Indians of the Late Archaic Period showed their presence in North America at 3000 B.P. at the earliest. By 1965, these dates were supplanted by evidence from archeological sites in England, New York, and Massachusetts. Then, because of a find at Yorkshire, England, the presence of dogs in Europe was set back to about 9000 B.P. The 1965 finds in North America set the date back to 5000 B.P. Within a few years these dates were eclipsed by studies that placed the dog in the western part of the United States and in the Middle East, south of the Black Sea, at even earlier times. A few years ago, the age of 12,000 B.P. in Israel, Iraq, and Iran, and 13,000 B.P. in Alaska became the references for the oldest dogs in the Old and New Worlds. These records soon may be eclipsed when carbon-14 dating of the Old Crow, Yukon, Canada, dogs is completed. The Yukon dogs might be thirty thousand years old!

While this oldest site is still under active study and the evidence is still accumulating, it does suggest the great antiquity for this friend of man. Will the tale of domestication of the dog continue backward in time even further? It may be so, to a limited degree, as sites in western China—so long closed to exploration—become the focus of renewed attention.

Additionally, the recent work along the Old Crow River suggests that a rich source of prehistoric evidence will emerge through new archeological work in Alaska and northwestern Canada. Future evidence will most likely confirm the trend in dating and the location of the archeological finds that point inexorably to Central Asia at about forty thousand years ago as the starting point for this relationship between man and dog. We also can expect some modest additions to the chronology for sites in North America that now date to 12,000 B.P. when man surged out of Alaska with his dogs to occupy anew the land below the glaciers.

Future finds, whether in China, Alaska, the Yukon, or western United States, will be the result of chance and the prepared mind of a person who studies the ancient record. Since man's early living sites were in caves or open country and because all known caves have been studied intensively over the past hundred years, it is now chance observation that controls the identification of prehistoric campgrounds across the vast continental land masses of the world.

Of course, large areas can be excluded from consideration because of the presence at earlier times of glaciers and inhospitable mountainous terrain that restricted access. Dry, barren regions reduced even further possible occupation areas. Except for a rapid traverse to a more favored hunting ground, these desert regions would be avoided by early man. It will be primarily along stream banks and lake shores, on bottom lands and in woodside clearings that the observant student of archeology will find the still-to-be-discovered living sites of early man.

It was just such an observation that led to the Old Crow excavation and the subsequent discovery of the dog at the Old Crow site in the Yukon. A paleontologist from the National Museum of Canada and his native guide, searching along the eroded banks of the Old Crow River, discovered at the edge of the river between the mouths of Johnson and Shaeffer Creeks, a long implement and a number of bone artifacts broken or otherwise altered by man. A large hand tool with a serrated edge for cutting flesh and scraping hides, and made from the tibia of a caribou, is dated at 27,000 B.P. These finds by Dr. C. R. Harington and P. Lord in 1966 have been followed by steady work at the site by many other researchers who have uncovered additional bone artifacts. These objects give a range of carbon-14 dates from 14,000 B.P. to 41,000 B.P.

The Old Crow sites are shown on the map of the northern hemisphere on page 38, along with some other sites of early man that have dates from 4000 B.P. to 100,000 B.P. The location of known sites with their earliest dates of occupation shows clearly the outward migration from northeast

Asia to Europe and the Americas. The maximum extent of the glacial ice advance at about 20,000 B.P. is also shown on page 38. This barrier blocked travel into North America while there were no restrictions for movement to the west across Eurasia.

The enlarged map of North America, shown on page 42, gives the names of locations and the dates for all currently recorded prehistoric sites where the remains of dogs occur prior to 1000 B.P. The record shows a long and continuous presence of dogs in North America and a gradual movement south and east from the Old Crow sites and the site below the glacial ice at Jaguar Cave, Idaho.

Even though the North American sites that have carbon-14 dated skeletal remains of dogs show an increasingly younger age as their distance from the northwest becomes greater, it is highly questionable to assume that the occupation of America by the Paleolithic population was so gradual. The dates shown on the map on page 42 indicate that the advance took place over thousands of years. Logic and the evidence from kill sites indicate a much more rapid movement. These vigorous and daring explorers literally must have burst forth into the vast fertile land after threading their way through the relatively narrow ice-free corridor east of the Canadian Rockies. Surely, these big game hunters and their families must have found a paradise. They encountered great game herds that were totally innocent of the danger from man. The new superpredators with their dogs killed the herds to have an abundance of food. Under such favorable circumstances, a group of one hundred individuals can multiply to a tremendous population within a few hundred years!

We can assume that the hunting groups, moving with the game herds, had natural checks on family size. There would be a high death rate because of the hazards of nature, living in the open, and the hunt. Even with a low birth rate of only 1.5 percent annually, or doubling in forty years, a hunting population of one person per square mile could be produced in a relatively short time. This indicates a population of twelve million over the region outside of Canada and the other glaciated areas. However, before even this density could be reached, such conditions would lead to overkill of the big game and ultimate extinction of most species. Additionally, many paleontologists believe that environmental change played an equally important part in the disappearance of the many Pleistocene fauna.

We know this to be a sound conclusion from the fossil record. Thirty-three genera of large animals, including horse, camel, tapir, mammoth, and saber-toothed tiger, to name just a few, vanished from the Americas

41

TRAIL CREEK
(~ 13,000)

OLD CROW
(30,000)

ICE FREE CORRIDOR
(Before 20,000
and after 10,000 Y. B. P.)

MAXIMUM EXTENT OF
GLACIAL ICE
(~ 20,000 Y. B. P.)

PORT AU CHOIX
(4,000)

JAGUAR
(10,400)

ITASCO
(7,500)

GENEVA
(4,500)

MARTHA'S
VINEYARDS
(4,200)

WRAY
(10,000)

KOSTER
(7,500)

VENTANA
(6,500)

GOVERNADOR
(4,000)

RODGERS
(7,400)

RUSSEL
(4,000)

**NORTH AMERICAN PREHISTORIC
DOG BURIAL SITES
WITH RADIOCARBON DATES**

within a relatively short time. This rapid depletion of the food supply would place a further check on population growth. Nevertheless, we know from kill-site evidence that the Paleolithic hunters swept across the Americas in a wave. Aided by dogs and fire, they must have decimated the larger wild game during their advance. In one thousand years they swept forward from the Arctic to Tierra del Fuego at the southern tip of South America. Paleolithic artifacts at Fells Cave, Southern Peru, dated at 10,700 B.P., are evidence of their advance.

The concept of overkill by prehistoric big game hunters to explain the rapid occupation of the Americas and the extinction of the Rancholabrean megafauna has its strongest advocate in Paul S. Martin. A professor of Geosciences at the University of Arizona, Martin has researched the issue extensively and in a recent study with James E. Mosimann presents analytical results that are based on very reasonable assumptions. Using a mathematical simulation that is programmed on a computer to simplify the calculations, the investigators postulate a variety of conditions for study. Their basic scenario involves the introduction of one hundred Paleo-Indians at Edmonton, Alberta, about 11,500 B.P. As stated in their paper in the May-June 1975 issue of "American Scientist," Martin and Mosimann described the probable events as follows:

> The hunters take an average of 13 animal units per year. One person in a family of four does most of the killing at an average rate of one animal per week, which is more meat than can be eaten; at least 50 percent of the meat is wasted. The hunting is easy; the tribe doubles every 20 years until local herds are depleted and fresh territory must be found. In 120 years, the Edmonton population grows to 5,409. It is concentrated on a front 59 miles deep at a density of 0.37 persons per square mile. Behind the front, the megafauna is exterminated. By 220 years, the front reaches Northern Colorado. The total population is just over 41,000. In the next 73 years, the front advances the remaining 1000 miles, attains a depth of 76 miles, and reaches a maximum of just over 100,000 people. Assuming an average life expectancy of 25 years, the total number of persons in the sweep from Edmonton to the Gulf of Mexico is less than 300,000. The front does not advance more than 20 miles in one year. In 293 years the hunters destroy a megafauna of 93 million animals.

The fact that not one but two breeds of dogs are identifiable in the debris at the 10,500-year-old living site at Jaguar Cave, Idaho, indicates that the big game hunters had more than stone pointed spears to subdue the wild game. This formidable combination of dog and man obviously would be successful.

Of course, as Martin states, "Basic to the model is the assumption that a relatively innocent prey was suddenly exposed to a new superpredator who preferred killing large animals to other outdoor activities." Their superpredator was obviously a spear-armed man and his dog. The battle was so swift in archeological time, a mere thousand years, that "there was little chance for preservation of either the extinct animals, the weapons used to kill them, or the bones of the hunters themselves."

This summary view must include dog as one of the hunters since at the Jaguar Cave occupation site of the Paleo-Indians, the oldest on record below the Wisconsin glacier, ancient mandibles and cranial fragments were found and carbon-14 dated at 10,370 B.P. If we accept Martin's assumptions and numbers for the Paleo-Indian population at about 250,000, and add the additional view that the hunters were aided by packs of dogs, it is not unreasonable to project a surprisingly large dog population. Of course, the number would fluctuate widely during the whelping season but was probably similar to the actual hunting population. Considering, on the average, one dog per hunter, we can project a dog population of about one hundred thousand during this greatest hunting period of all time.

Jaguar Cave Dog

In the summer of 1961 during a hike of exploration in the western slopes of the Beaverhead Mountains in southeastern Idaho, a young archeologist was drawn to a favored spot in Indian Head Canyon. During exploratory excavations at the base of a low cliff, she discovered a cave behind accumulated rubble. This was a rare event in prehistoric archeology, for Jaguar Cave, as it was subsequently called, ultimately gave forth a fascinating glimpse of the life style of the first Paleo-Indians. More interesting for our purposes, Jaguar Cave proved to be the home of two different types of dogs—as judged by the skeletal remains that were unearthed at this site.

In the succeeding summers, Dr. Hind Sadek-Kooros, who found the cave, and her associates from Harvard and Idaho State Universities, excavated the roughly rectangular floor of the cave over an eight by eleven meter area to reach bedrock. When first discovered, the cave was filled with pieces of rock from the ceiling, dirt carried in by wind and the occupants, and several tens of thousands of fragments of animals bones.

Most of the bones had been split deliberately by the Paleo-Indians in order to reach the marrow for food. Chipped stone artifacts, charcoal from many fires, and a few bone pieces with evidence of workmanship also were recovered. Two charcoal samples showed a carbon-14 age of 10,370 plus or minus 350 years and 11,580 plus or minus 250 years. These dates were determined from charcoal positioned near the top and near the bottom of the debris and show that the cave was open to Indian Head Canyon at least twelve thousand years ago, and that it was filled with debris and sealed at sometime less than ten thousand years ago. It was occupied more or less continuously during this two thousand year period, for the bones were distributed throughout the one and a half meters of fill that covered the floor.

Modern scientific methods can even tell us something about the environmental conditions that prevailed while these early people and their dogs used Jaguar Cave as their home. Limestone, the basic rock formation that surrounds the cave, was analyzed by thermoluminescence measurements to determine the previous mean high temperature of the sample under study. Tests on the limestone rock beneath the floor, above the entrance, in the roof, and at the back of the cave were measured to give information about the relative temperatures at these locations. The original floor temperature was higher than that for the rock above the entrance, indicating that the cave interior, even before rotting debris would raise surface temperatures, was measurably warmer than the outside temperature.

Similarly high temperatures at the cave roof and rear wall show the effects of human occupation and fires in the cave. The coolest temperature recorded, that for the rock above the entrance, relates to the outdoor environment during the final retreat of the Wisconsin ice sheet in the mid-continent and the glaciers of the western high plateau region.

Just sixteen kilometers from Jaguar Cave were many glaciers on the slopes of the Lemhi Mountains. Jaguar Cave, shielded from the sun by a high ridge on the southern side of Indian Head Canyon and by extensive cloud cover to the southwest over the Lemhi Mountains during summer afternoons, was a warm haven for the men and their families who hunted the wild beasts near the end of Wisconsin time.

On the cave floor, at the same level and square as the hearth dated at 10,370 B.P., were found two paired mandibles and a single jaw bone of *Canis familiaris*. As investigated by Barbara Lawrence, each of the paired jaws has the lower portion and most of the ascending ramus broken away and each has but one tooth, the second molar. The right jaw bone of the two is shown in the upper left of the illustration on page 28. As noted by

Lawrence in judging the bones, "The jaws, as well as being shortened, are wide-spread in typical dog fashion." She states also that "the ratio of width across the tooth rows at the second molar to the length of the tooth row is diagnostic of dog rather than coyote or wolf."

Lawrence further observes, "It is possible to say that the animals were rather short-nosed with a broad palate, and since a short, broad nose in dogs is correlated with a steep forehead, one can further say that the animals in question had this most doglike of all characters well developed." Later in the study, she reports, "Both suggest that the range of variation in these early animals was from a small, short-nosed animal with a broad palate and rather large braincase to a slightly larger, longer-skulled form."

At the same level in Jaguar Cave as the previously described dogs were uncovered equally old cranial and jaw fragments of a considerably larger animal. Because only broken pieces were available for study, the task of identification was particularly challenging. In a separate effort, Lawrence compared these skeletal remains with a portion of a dog skull from the Itasca Bison Site in Minnesota (7500 B.P.), with material found at a considerably later site in nearby Birch Creek Valley, Idaho (4500 B.P.), and with wolf and coyote diagnostic measurements. She reported that "the skull and jaw of the largest Jaguar Cave animals are very similar to certain recent Eskimo dogs in the collection of the Peabody Museum."

The skull shapes deduced by Lawrence for the two Jaguar Cave dogs can be compared reasonably to the representative skulls shown on page 47. The small Jaguar Cave dog was probably similar to the Kentucky shell-midden dog, while, as Lawrence concluded, the larger dog resembled the modern Arctic Dog. These skulls were part of the study by Haag and are typical of those for the periods under study.

The presence of two sizes of dogs at the same time so long ago is of particular interest. Prior to this discovery and analysis, it was concluded by earlier investigators that there had been a gradual increase in size of dogs through prehistoric time. With the uncovering at Jaguar Cave of both small and large dogs, there is now firm evidence that smallness is not necessarily a characteristic of the earliest dogs in America. The differences are so great that the process of domestication must have been underway for many prior thousands of years. Dog teeth from Trail Creek and jaw fragments from Old Crow further support this conclusion. The Old Crow and Jaguar Cave animals, so different in form, are evidence that at least two distinctly different types of dogs traveled with early man through the western corridor to hunt big game and subsequently to multiply across the new land south of the great ice fields.

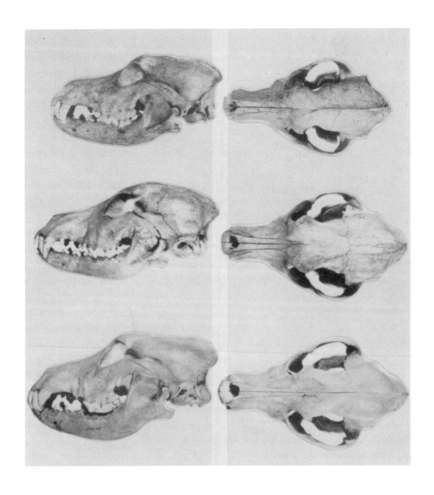

Representative dog skulls from Kentucky shell heaps (top), Northwest Coast shell heaps (center), and the Arctic (bottom). The Kentucky dog skull is about two inches shorter and one inch narrower than the skull of the Arctic dog. (From Haag, 1948.)

Koster Farm Dog

On a sunny day in 1965, Dr. Stuart Struever and a professional associate were scouting the southern Illinois countryside for likely living sites of Archaic and Woodland Indians. Having walked across some plowed fields to a bluff that overlooked a recessed area along the lower Illinois River, they looked down at the property and buildings of the Koster Farm. Here, thought Struever, was just the location for an ancient Indian village. A small stream cut across the low land from its start at a spring at the base of the bluff, to join the Illinois River at a distance. Sheltered from the harsh prevailing winds that blow across the flat country above the bluff, the Koster Site would be an ideal location. The record of many thousands of years of occupation might be just below the soil along the meandering brook. The land was built up to the present level by the deposit of fine wind-blown soil from regions to the west as it eddied over the bluff and settled into the recess.

Moved by a vision of discovery of prehistoric relics and with the generous permission of Mr. and Mrs. Theodore Koster, what was to become the biggest archeological dig in middle America got underway. With the aid of local residents, many associates, and students from Northwestern University, by the summer of 1970 the dig covered an area of over an acre and was down to eight meters below the original surface. In one of the excavation sections on a bright day in the summer of 1970, there was great excitement as a shout from a young, dirty, and hot woman student of archeology rang across the site. The full skeleton of an ancient dog was uncovered that day! In time it would gain fame as the Koster dog, one of the oldest interred dogs in America.

The dog skeleton was unearthed lying on its side in a fire pit at the eleventh cultural horizon of the site. Sometime later, its age was set at about 7000 B.P. as determined from the carbon-14 dating of charred wood found with the burial. In size, the Koster dog is about the same as the small Jaguar Cave dog and a dog discovered at the Rodgers Shelter Site in Missouri by R. B. McMillan in 1966. The Rodgers dog also had been interred. It was unearthed in a shallow pit and had been covered with a pile of small stones by its Archaic Indian owners. Carbon-14 dating of carbonized wood from the same level as the dog gave a measurement of 7540 B.P. plus or minus 170.

The Koster dog had been placed on top of a fire after death. The left front foot and other associated animal remains were burned and discolored by the residual fire before it was extinguished. Since none of the bones of the dog were cut or broken purposely, one can assume that the burial was part of a ritual. These burials at Koster Farm and Rodgers

48

Shelter show the important position held by dog in the life of the Paleo-Indian in America. So valued was dog to man that by at least 7500 B.P., the same type of special care afforded to deceased members of the tribe was also given to the hunting companions. The methods of honoring the dead dog by erecting a stone cairn over the body or by cremation require considerable forethought and overt action. Digging a pit for the burial, gathering stones or dry wood for the fire, moving the body to a burial position, and, finally, covering it with stones or dirt are all physical acts of a special sort. Archeological evidence shows these events to be related uniquely to dog burials and thereby can be classed as an example of acts with religious significance for man.

The Koster dog has been thoroughly studied and measured by Dr. Frederick C. Hill. The well-preserved skeleton shows the dog to have been an adult with teeth worn as a result of diet and age. Hill states, "The Koster dog, similar to the Rodgers Shelter canid, was between 42 and 50 cm tall at the shoulders, approximately the height of present-day fox terriers." The large head and teeth of the Koster dog make its form somewhat out of proportion to its slight frame. Also, the short tail is a peculiar feature which may have some special significance. These aspects of the skeleton are easily distinguished in the illustration on page 50, which shows the remains shortly after they were unearthed. Measurements by Hill show the occipital length to be 170 mm, the maximum skull width to be 47.5 mm, the distance from the canine to the last molar to be 75.8 mm, and the tibia length to be 132 mm.

Port au Choix Dog

While most archeological sites are discovered during diligent field work by dedicated investigators, important living or burial sites of Paleo-Indians or Archaic Indians have been discovered on rare occasions by people engaged in various types of construction. During the building of homes or commercial buildings the use of earth-moving or excavating equipment usually is required to prepare the site for the construction of suitable foundations. Such activity displaces the earth to reveal the subsurface sediments and any occupation sites that may be present. Through this type of accidental encounter, a new view has emerged of the Archaic Indians of the North Atlantic Provinces. For example, in 1967 in the town of Port au Choix, northwestern Newfoundland, during the digging for foundations for a theater and billiard parlor on an ancient beach that overlooks an embayment from the Gulf of Saint Lawrence, the work was halted abruptly after a bulldozer cut through a mass of human bones and Indian artifacts surrounded by red ochre. The owner

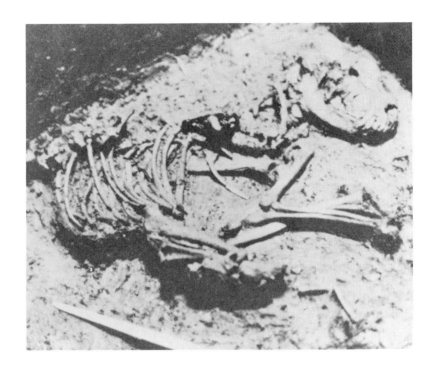

An adult Terrier-like dog with a large head, buried in a fire pit by Middle Archaic Indians at the Koster site in southwestern Illinois. Dated about 7500 B.P. (Hill, 1972.)

of the property, Mr. Felix Gould, recognized the importance of these finds and stopped all work until an archeologist from Memorial University of Newfoundland could arrive to investigate the remains. Within a few days James A. Tuck announced his findings—an ancient undisturbed burial site of prehistoric people.

With the aid of students and professional investigators and with permission of Mr. Gould, an extensive program of controlled excavations was completed during succeeding summers. The numerous test pits and trenches revealed three distinct Archaic Indian cemeteries. A total of one hundred clearly identifiable graves of adults and children, plus a great quantity of hand-worked objects, were unearthed.

One grave contained the remains of an adult male and an adult female placed on their sides facing each other and an infant less than two years old held in the man's arms. On a layer of sand overlying the human skeletons were the bones of two sizable dogs. These animals were clearly interred as ceremonial offerings to accompany the family after death. This burial was the subject of careful study by Tuck. Human bone processed for carbon-14 dating revealed an age of 3930 B.P. plus or minus 130. Together with radio carbon dates from wood charcoal samples, it was concluded that the Port au Choix cemetery was used for about eight hundred years and that the joint burial of the two dogs and the three humans occurred after about two hundred years of site use.

At about the same time as the Port au Choix occupation, but a thousand miles to the west in the northern portion of the Finger Lake region in New York State, groups of Laurentian Archaic Indians also were burying dogs and masters together. These sites were studied extensively by a team of archeologists led by Dr. William A. Ritchie. In the refuse at a site at Geneva, New York, "seven flexed burials of a small terrier-sized dog" were unearthed. Here and at a Frontenac Island site, burial practices were similar to those at Port au Choix. Ritchie reported the dog finds as follows: "An affectionate regard for the dog is indicated by separate burials in six cases; while recognition of his invaluable services to the hunter seems a logical inference from the fact that in all other instances (6) save one, an infant, dog burials were the accompaniment of males, usually provided with hunting and other equipment."

Ritchie identified the Frontenac Island dogs as two breeds, one of Terrier-size and the other of Collie-size. Tuck compared the Port au Choix dogs with the large Frontenac Island dogs and judged them to be similar. He concluded that the Port au Choix dogs were considerably different from "the skeletons of Eskimo sled dogs in use today."

Examination of the graves and skeletal remains of the Port au Choix dogs has allowed reconstruction of events at the time of burial. The dogs were interred about two feet below the surface of the beach sand. After death, they had been placed on a bed of sand about one foot deep that overlaid the man, women, and child. The grave was about six feet in circumference and about four feet deep. The dogs were fully articulated and "complete to the last caudal vertebrae and the sesamoid bones of the feet." Both had been placed on their sides with legs slightly bent in a sleeping position. Tuck reported further, "The younger and larger of the two male dogs showed no evidence of the cause of death although it may have been strangled, while the older dog was killed by a blow to the left side of the head as evidenced by a depressed fracture of the bones, including the zygoma." Since, in all populations, most individuals are right-handed, it is fair to assume that the deadly blow was delivered by a stone axe while the dog was attentively and innocently looking at his assailant.

Tuck judged these dogs to have weighed between forty-five and fifty-five pounds. Since the muscle attachment areas were well developed, it can be assumed that they were working dogs although not necessarily used to drag sleds. One also can assume that these dogs were constant companions of the males during hunting expeditions. This is evident from the grave goods buried with the dog and master in this instance and from the many other examples of common dog-man burials among the Archaic Indians in New York State. We can almost see the pair after the killing of a large bear, deer, or caribou. The dead animal would be tied to both as they dragged the carcass to the campsite. Later, the choice portions of meat that remained after the feast would be gathered, together with other family possessions. The dog, trudging along with the stalwart hunter, his wife, and child, surely must have pack-carried the load to the next campsite.

From the condition of the skeletal remains that have been unearthed at the various living and burial sites prior to the time of the Port au Choix people, we can observe radical differences in the man-dog relationship. At the earliest period of man's entrance into North America, set by the Jaguar Cave finds, cracked bones and skull fragments of dogs were thrown among the other refuse in the living area. Little regard for the dead is evident. In fact, the remains often show signs of dogs having been food for the group. The first dog burials occurred about 7000 B.P. and show a sensitivity to the loss of the animal by its owner. Laid in a shallow pit or on a smoldering fire, these ancient dogs were a special concern of the tribe even after death. Buried in the loose middens and shell-heaps near the living site (such as at Rodgers Shelter), they could remain near to give symbolic aid or comfort. Still later, as evident at Port au Choix and Frontenac Island, a relationship was common that bound man and dog even after death.

By 4000 B.P. the hunter and his dog were buried together to ensure continuing companionship and teamwork in the hereafter. While the earlier hunter buried his dead dog, now the surviving family members gave a fatal blow to the dog so it could join its dead master. The Port au Choix mass burial of two dogs and three humans shows this new course of action in time of tragedy. With the death of this young family group in some unknown but no doubt sorrowful way, it was left to their friends to dig the burial pit and to kill the dogs. Such practices required the attention and work of all members of the remaining small community. With primitive hand tools the effort would be arduous. The burial may even have had to be left, if in the winter, until spring warmth once again thawed the ground. The use of red ochre, the careful positioning of the humans with their prized possessions, the killing and interment of their favorite dogs to guard the deceased forever, symbolized the ultimate man-dog relationship.

Above: An elaborate burial of two dogs above the grave of an adult man and woman at the Locus II site in Port au Choix, Newfoundland, is carbon-14 dated at about 4400 B.P. (Tuck, 1970.)

Below: Two of the four skulls of domestic dogs found at Port au Choix, of a size between a Terrier and a Retriever. The larger may have weighed between forty-five and fifty-five pounds. (Tuck, 1976.)

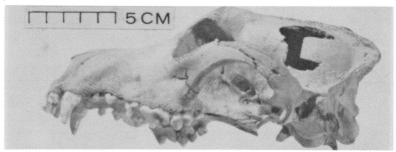

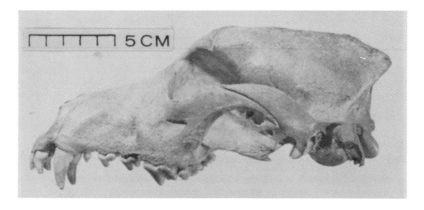

Dogs in Rock Art

In addition to observations of bones and buried artifacts in the earth-fill and shell-heaps of prehistoric living sites and hunting camps, it also is natural to look at rock art for evidence of prehistoric dogs. Painted or engraved on the smooth surfaces of rock outcroppings or cave walls are many thousands of picture writings by American Indians. It is surprising that the content, styles, and meaning of this vast array of rock pictures is unknown to most people and considered a heritage of our past by but a few.

Compared with the cave art of southern France and northern Spain, which commands world-wide interest, American prehistoric rock art attracts little attention. If it were not for a few dedicated students of American prehistory, much of the record of this treasure would have been lost through casual destruction or vandalism. Fortunately, the work of the original American investigator in this field, Colonel Garrick Mallery, published in 1886, has been added to recently by specialists such as R. F. Heizer, C. Meighan, M. Baumhoff, D. Gebhard, D. Scott, and Campbell Grant. The work by Mallery contains more than twelve hundred picture-writings by American Indians. The books by Grant contain an interpretation of more than fifteen hundred rock art pictures; his latest contains a collection selected carefully from the many thousands that are recorded across America.

The task of reporting all such works is beyond the scope of this book, but there are enough examples to reach certain conclusions about this pictorial history. The rock art pictures are classified from oldest to youngest as naturalistic, stylized, or abstract. The oldest examples of rock art are in the Great Basin of the Northwest and the Southwest. Designs frequently are superimposed over each other and most of the oldest are naturalistic scenes of various types of animals. In the naturalistic pecked designs, mountain sheep appear most often and occur over a very large area of the west. Other animals such as the buffalo and deer are shown, as are the tracks of bear.

In the Great Basin region of the Coso Mountain Range there are numerous petroglyphs of dogs with bighorn sheep. Frequently they are shown pursuing the sheep and attacking from front and rear in the act of holding the wild animals at bay. Some of these scenes are judged by Grant to be dated as far back as 3000 B.P. and were made by western Shoshoni Indians.

The illustration on page 57 shows four petroglyphs of dogs, out of the two hundred twenty-five on the basaltic rocks of the Sheep, Petroglyph, and Remegrade Canyons of the Coso Peak area which were recorded by Grant. It is easy to distinguish the dogs from sheep and deer because the dogs have long tails of two different types. Most rock carvings show the dogs with straight tails angled upward at about forty-five degrees from the line of the back, while a few are shown with exceptionally long tails that curve over the back and almost reach the head.

The densest concentration of rock art occurs in the north end of Petroglyph Canyon, where there are about thirty-seven hundred drawings. In this group there are seventy-one dogs and over two thousand sheep. The dogs are of the straight-tailed variety and, based on their association with the sheep, undoubtedly were used in driving the prey past hunters in ambush blinds. The sheep were then killed either by the atlatl or the bow and arrow, and, since both weapons are shown in drawings at this site, they thereby date the work to about 2000 B.P. during the Transitional Period.

Drawings of dogs with the long curved tails occur in an isolated small canyon about ten miles east of the main concentration in the Coso Range. They date from about 1500 B.P. during the Late Period of occupation by the prehistoric Shoshoneans. As seen on page 57, they were longer, lower dogs than those drawn at an earlier time in the Sheep, Horse, and Petroglyph Canyons. Although the tail may be an artful exaggeration, there can be no doubt of the existence during these periods of two distinctly different varieties of dogs for driving sheep to be slaughtered by their Indian owners.

A large action scene of a different sort, recorded by Mallery, is shown on page 59. A line of animals, with lines of dogs on either side and handlers interspersed, is carved on a rock in New Mexico. This special scene was described by W. H. Holmes of the Bureau of Ethnology in 1885.

The examples occur on the Rio San Juan about 10 miles below the Rio La Plata near the New Mexico and Colorado border. A low line of bluffs, composed of light-colored massive sandstones that break down in great smooth faced blocks, rise from the river level and sweep toward the north. Each of these great blocks has offered a very

56

Examples of rock art from the California Coso Range, showing two varieties of dog attacking sheep. These petroglyphs, dated from 1500 and 2000 B.P., were made by Western Shoshoni hunters. (Grant, 1967.)

tempting tablet to the graves of the primitive artist, and many of them contain curious and interesting inscriptions . . . . With very few exceptions the engraving bears undoubted evidence of age . . . . The most striking group consists of a great procession of men, birds, beasts and fanciful figures. The whole picture as placed up on a rock is highly spirited and the idea of a general movement toward the right, skillfully portrayed . . . . The figures forming the main body of the procession appear to be tied together in a continuous line, and in form resemble one living creature about as little as another. Many of the smaller figures above and below are certainly intended to represent dog, while a number of men are stationed about here and there as if to keep the procession in order.

The oldest petroglyphs that show dog in North America are in New Mexico, Utah, and Idaho. The elaborate scene on page 59 was chipped in sandstone to a depth of one-fourth to one-half an inch and is about thirty feet long. The surface has a dark patina, or "desert varnish," over the original lighter rock as a result of aging in the dry climate. Holmes stated, "New figures as occur are quite easily distinguished both by the freshness of the chipped surfaces and by the designs themselves." Donald Martin has studied western rock art and the problem of dating the work. His experiments show that desert varnish is quickly washed off in a few rainy seasons, indicating that the age of such petroglyphs in desert regions is no older than the last period of unusual rainfall. In the southwest the decline of the last great rainy period was about three thousand to four thousand years ago. By such reasoning it is assumed that the Rio San Juan scene is probably about three thousand years old.

Although the exact age of rock art cannot now be determined, the scenes show clearly the roles of the dog in prehistoric time. In the Rio San Juan scene, on each side of the line of large animals that could be bison, are arrayed twenty dogs of very small to medium size. The scene conveys the impression that the large animals are being herded by the dogs toward some distant area. Holmes conjectures as follows, "This picture may represent the migration of a tribe or family or the trophies of victory." Whatever the purpose, there is no doubt of the important role displayed for the dogs. From the scenes in the Coso Range, it is clear that dogs were used to track and corral bighorn sheep for their Indian owners. No doubt with these hunting aids, the killing of wild animals for meat and hide would have been measurably improved.

At about the same time that the Archaic Indian of the Southwest carved the herding scene with dogs, and the primitive hunter made the

Above: Procession of wild animals and herd dogs engraved into the face of a massive sandstone rock by Archaic Indians. These petroglyphs are from the canyon of the Rio San Juan near the New Mexico and Colorado border. (Mallery, 1896.)

Below: Early Bronze Age (ca. 3500 B.P.) hunter with his dogs, shown in a rock carving discovered in 1927 in Haltane, Bohuslan, Sweden. This petroglyph of ten dogs, all of a type, with long bodies and large floppy ears, is the earliest record of a pack of dogs with common features.

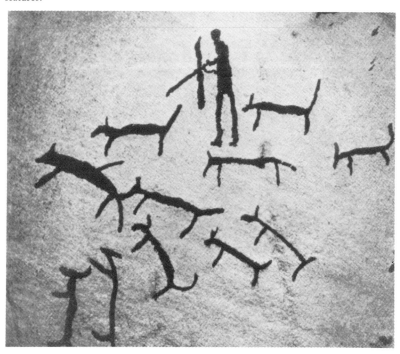

59

hunting scenes of bighorn sheep and dogs, an artist on a sunny slope in Haltane, Sweden, was carving on a rock a record of his recent feat. He is shown killing a wild animal with bow and arrow. This vivid scene, shown on page 59, includes ten dogs in states of excitement charging after the wounded beast, ears flying, tails up, all hard on the heels of the prey. This type of scene could just as easily have been made by the American Indian chieftain who was laid to rest with his two prized hunting dogs at Port au Choix, Newfoundland.

The Haltane rock carving, measuring about two by three feet, appears on a flat rock at ground level on a farm in the Kville Parish of Bohuslan. The figures are sharp and the composition appears to have been made all at one time during the Early Bronze Age, about three thousand years ago. Compared to the Rio San Juan carving shown on page 59, the Haltane scene shows only one type of dog, of about the same size, with longish bodies. The Haltane dogs are two-legged stick figures, while in the San Juan scene the dogs are four-legged and are shown as outlines. Both scenes show distinctly the dogs in action and in an important role with their owners. These are excellent art works in addition to being important sources of information about dogs in Europe and North America, and both were made at about the same time. They represent the earliest known rock art containing dogs and are far superior to others of the next period when the Indian art is stylized, and, therefore, difficult to identify. Of course among the most recent abstract rock art scenes, not a dog, nor very much else, can be distinguished, just as in modern abstract art!

Prehistoric Varieties

The variation of prehistoric dogs that is evident in the numerous archeological finds that span the twelve thousand years since the end of the last glacial period, can be explained as deliberate selection for breeding of the physically unusual animal or to satisfy a human need. The first springs from the genetic variability within the gene pool of the species. The rich gene pool of the dog can result in considerable differences in form. When early man protected the wild wolf/dog, there occurred a relaxation of natural pressures that had led previously to the destruction of any variant with physical limitations. With dog a part of man's environment and protected, puppies that possessed some odd feature or unique physical characteristic might survive. These minor variations were probably most important in changing wolf to dog during the early period of association with man. In time, as the man/dog

Early Woodland Indian dog burial at the Pratt site on Martha's Vineyard, radiocarbon dated at about 2500 B.P. (Ritchie, 1969.)

61

relationship grew, it is probable that considerably more variation in dogs resulted from changes in human social organization.

Man's continuing search for aids to his survival and for means to satisfy personal and group needs, resulted in new dog varieties. In the earliest of relationships the wolf/dog served to alert the tribe to the presence of human or animal predators. Later, the role of hunter was established and in time required special dog features that depended on the type of game being sought. Still later, as seen in the rock art from southwest Colorado and New Mexico, the characteristics of dogs that permitted the control of a herd of animals were exploited to produce yet another type. The skeletal remains confirm the changes that took place.

The size of the prehistoric dogs ranged from about 30 cm at the withers to over 50 cm. As adults, their skull length varied from 11 cm to 21 cm and the width across the zygomatic arch varied from 8.5 cm to 12 cm. Nostril width variation was considerable, indicating sharp-nosed dogs, and broad-nosed dogs with special scenting ability. Of note is variation in the angle of the nose and head junction; dogs with a straight profile and others with a very distinct "stop" have been discovered.

We know nothing about the body size or type of coat of the many interred prehistoric dogs because flesh, skin, and hair do not usually survive burial in the earth. However, some inference can be drawn by noting the development of the attachment areas for ligaments and muscles. Some skeletons show these areas well developed and indicate the use of the dog in hard labor as a pack animal or to drag sleds. It is difficult to identify the physical form of the dog from the appearance and size of the skull and bones. Using the skeletons of modern dogs for comparison, several investigators note that there were dogs similar to Toy Terriers, Collies, Eskimo Dogs, Spaniels, and wolf-like Shepherds.

Dr. William C. Haag studied the bones of about 300 dogs from many archeological sites in North America. Of the group, 174 were from the Archaic Indian period shell mounds in Kentucky and Alabama; 27 from the Basketmaker and Pueblo Indian periods of the Southwest; 7 from northeast coast shell heaps (pages 61 and 63); 39 from Saint Laurence Island near the Bering Strait; 18 from Kodiak Island in the Aleutians; 19 from Greenland; 10 from the Middle West Woodland Indian Period; and 12 from the Mississippi Indian Period. Haag distinguished several breeds even though the number in each group proved too small for very refined analysis. A study of Southwestern dogs, by Dr. Harold S. Colton, included 67 specimens from the Museum of Northern Arizona that were compared with 43 specimens of the Archaic Indian dogs, most of which were from Kentucky and Alabama. Colton concludes that the Alabama

Middle Woodland Indian dog burial at the Kipp Island site in Central New York. This burial, radiocarbon dated at about 1200 B.P., shows some care for the animal.

dogs were a little larger than the average from Kentucky, and that there were two distinctly different varieties in Arizona.

A recent report by Dr. Steven D. Emslie of his study of twenty whole or partial Indian dog skeletons from archeological sites in Mancos Canyon, south of Mesa Verde National Park, confirms Colton's conclusion about the Indian dogs of the Southwest. He states, "Three types of Southwestern Indian dogs are now recognized based on osteological measurements. These three types are the small, short-faced, and large Indian dogs." The short-faced Indian dog, along with a large Collie-like dog, is available for viewing in its entirety as a mummified specimen. These two dogs, discovered by S. J. Guernsey and A. V. Kidder and reported in 1921, are from the Kayenta, Arizona, region and are shown on page 65. These fifteen-hundred-year-old dogs are included in an exhaustive study of native Indian dogs made by Dr. Glover M. Allen of the Harvard College Museum of Comparative Zoology in 1920.

The larger is a long-haired animal the size of a small collie, with erect ears and long bushy tail. The hair is still in good condition and though now a light golden color, with cloudings of dark brown, it may in life have been darker. The other dog is a much smaller, black and white individual, about the size of a terrier, with short, but not close, shaggy coat, erect ears, and long full-haired tail. Its muzzle is rather short and stubby in contrast to the fine slender muzzle of the other Indian dogs of about the same size. I have called this the short-nosed Indian dog.

The beautiful pottery and statuary of the Mesoamerican civilizations is yet another source of information about the status of the dog in prehistoric times. The area comprising principally Mexico and the Yucatan Peninsula was first occupied before the Wisconsin Glacial Period. Evidence of man is found in the Valseguillo region southeast of Mexico City at this earliest authenticated archeological find in America. Much later, after the world-wide temperature increase around 9000 B.P., the Mesoamerican Paleo-Indians slowly gained control over their environment by the domestication of plants and with the aid of their one domesticated animal, the dog. By 3500 B.P. village life was recorded in small clay sculptures of native huts within which are figures of people and dogs. Of special interest is the small clay figurine of a nude female and dog that dates to this period. It was found at Tlatilco, a site northwest of Mexico City, and is the earliest likeness of a dog from the Americas that has been discovered to date. Only older are the small figurines of dogs with curly tails found at Jarmo, Iraq, and dated to about 10,000 B.P.

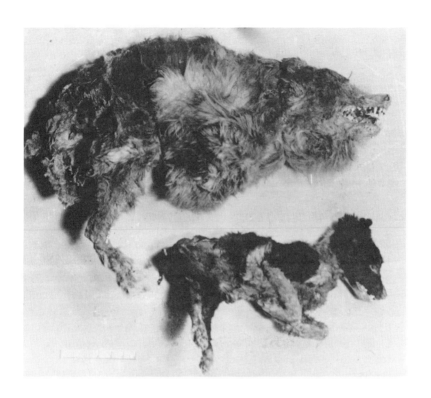

A Long-haired Pueblo Dog and a smaller black and white Short-nosed Indian Dog. Found at White Cave, Marsh Pass, Arizona, in a mummified state, at a living site of Basketmaker II Indians dated about 1500 B.P. (Guernsey and Kidder, 1921.)

The Tlatilco dog, shown on page 67, could be the Xoloitzcuintli, or common hairless dog, famous as a food of the Mesoamericans. The dog, when compared to the woman, appears to be about eight inches high at the withers. The sucking position of the animal leads to the view that it is a puppy. The practice of nourishing young dogs with milk from women may have been a common way to ensure survival of all the pups born to each small canine. It certainly would have been a prudent practice if the pups were one day to serve as a meal for an Indian priest or noble.

Other statues of plump domesticated dogs, shown on page 68, are from the Early Classic Period of the Colima civilization, about 2000 B.P. These beautifully shaped hairless dogs, sculptured in highly polished red clay, are grave furniture, symbolizing food or companionship. Placed at the feet of a deceased person, it was believed that the dog could provide warmth and also guide a lost soul between this world and the next.

A figure similar in form and size to the Colima dogs is the burial effigy of a Mississippi Culture Indian of Tennessee shown on page 69. This dog has a head shaped surprisingly like that of the modern Chihuahua but a tail that is quite different; the modern Chihuahua tail can be looped only to just touch the back.

A surprising range of dog types is evident when one compares the clay effigy burial dog, the two 1500-year-old mummified dogs from Arizona, and the 10,400-year-old dog skeletal remains from Jaguar Cave. Lawrence describes one of the Jaguar Cave dogs as a "small, short-nosed animal with a broad palate and rather large brain case to a slightly larger, long skulled form" and the other larger dog as "very similar to certain recent Eskimo dogs in the collection of the Museum of Comparative Zoology." Allen describes one mummified dog as Terrier-like, the other as Collie-like. The 7000-year-old pointed-nose dog unearthed at Koster Farm is reported by Hill to be "similar to the present-day Fox Terrier."

At the Port au Choix archeological site, Tuck noted that the 4000-year-old dogs "may have weighed between 45 and 55 pounds" and in size and proportions were similar to a Retriever. The very small dogs from Mesoamerica, as shown by clay statuary, are of still another type.

From these descriptions, and the results of studies of hundreds of other skeletons, we know with certainty that since prehistoric time when dogs, associated with man, reached the New World from Asia, the canine species we know as the dog had evolved into a highly variable species with numerous distinctly different varieties and subgroups. We also know that many of these varieties were still here in America five hundred years ago to greet the first explorers from Europe at the beginning of the new era in American history.

Earliest known figure of a dog discovered in America. From Tlatilco, Mexico, and dated about 3700 B.P. The relative size of the woman indicates the young dog in life was about eight inches high at the withers. The Xoloitzcuintli, or common hairless dog, was used as a foot warmer and as food.

Above and below: Plump domesticated dog replicas used as burial furniture from the Colima civilization of Mexico, dated about 2000 B.P.

Burial effigy in the form of a dog from the Mississippi Culture Indians, dated about 1500 B.P. Note curly tail and similarity in form to plump domesticated dog from Colima Culture of Mexico.

69

Skin tepee of Assiniboine chief, with three dog travois propped together and a Plains-Indian Dog in harness.

70

American Indians and Their Dogs

Since there were so many Indian tribes that inhabited the Americas during the time of discovery by European explorers, it is customary to use various strategies that permit the identification of groups of tribes to facilitate study and discussion. Groupings have been based on language, tribal customs, religious practice, geographical location, and various physical characteristics such as shape of head. Tribes that exhibit similar values, habits, skills, material culture and social organization, and share a similar environment, can be identified as a cultural group. The grouping of tribes of similar culture is most convenient for studies of the social aspects of Indians and can be used advantageously in our study of the dogs of the Indians. Ten cultural areas can be identified as encompassing all the tribes within the boundaries of the United States and Canada. It is reasonable to divide the area occupied by the various tribes to the south of the United States into four cultural areas. These are the Caribbean, Middle America, and two in South America. Of the last, one is the Inca Cultural Group and the other includes all tribes to Tierra del Fuegia at the southernmost portion. To the north of the Mexican border the ten cultural groupings occupy land areas with fairly uniform geographical features and climate. The North Portion Cultural Groups can be identified as Arctic, Sub-Arctic, and Northwest Coast. Across Middle America are the Eastern Woodland, Plains, Plateau, and Great Basin Cultural Groups, while across the southern portion of the United States, cultural groups of the Southeast, Southwest, and California Indians are identifiable.

The tribes of each cultural group displayed numerous similarities in life style, principally because of the dependence of the tribes on the natural surroundings. Since the climate and topography of the land occupied by each group is quite different, there also are some sharp differences between tribes that lived in the various areas and comprised the cultural groups. Since the boundaries of these groupings cannot be drawn sharply, some features of Indian life overlap into adjacent areas of the groups. Additionally, people of the same language family were often located in more than one cultural group because of early migrations and

71

intermixing of tribes. Therefore, it is not uncommon to find in the same cultural group tribes with entirely different languages. The Southwestern Cultural Group was most varied, with tribes that conversed in four of the six basic Indian languages of North America while the Indians of the California Cultural Group used six basic languages. Additionally, the basic languages were subdivided into many local dialects so that it was common for some tribes in a cultural group to use a dialect incomprehensible to other tribes in the same group.

There are still other reasons why tribes of a cultural group are not entirely uniform in all social aspects. No scheme for marking boundaries can be entirely correct. Also, tribal groups moved between geographical areas as the result of war, famine, and trade. The response to such shifting of the population was a transference of cultural features across boundaries, and, occasionally, the introduction of a new basic language. This transference is seen most vividly in the existence of dogs of a similar variety in more than one cultural group. In the study of Indian dogs, it is evident that the same type of dog was bred by Indians in a number of adjacent areas. In other cases, a certain type of Indian dog was kept only by the tribes within a single area. The dispersal of a breed, whether quite locally or over a wide area, was linked most closely to the living conditions of the Indians and the climate of the region. This distribution of the various breeds of Indian dogs offers an additional criteria for the demarcation of cultural areas.

Because of the great importance of the dog to the livelihood and, at times, the very survival of certain groups, it is generally agreed that a dog culture existed in many portions of America prior to the introduction and propagation of the horse. In this chapter, we will use the pictorial and written record of the early explorers to help us identify and describe the different types and breeds of dogs of each of the Indian cultural groups. The uses and roles of the dog in Indian society will be explained, and information will be presented about the raising, training, and breeding of dogs as conveyed by the records and customs. Important sources of information about the physical appearance of Indian dogs are the sketches and paintings of artists that lived with the tribal groups during the early 1800s. A search in the art libraries reveals many examples that can be studied and compared.

Although great diversity in physical appearance, language, and social customs still occurs in the American Indians, even the average person of today thinks that all Indians are alike. Over the years, two opposite views prevail. One holds the Indian as a noble, generous, and chivalrous race far above the usual standards of American society; the other places

Indians at the level of brutes without feeling or honor. Despite vast numbers of studies by anthropologists and other scientists, and extensive literature about the Indians, misconceptions continue because of our inability to view the Indian with anything but European-based values.

Our concepts of land ownership, saving for the future, individual competitiveness, year-round work, and land usage are still unacceptable to many Indians. Their attachment to the land, reverence for nature, and holding man as a brother to all living things are strange to most modern Americans. The dogs of the American Indians are also strange. They too suffer from a stereotypical view held by modern Americans. They are either totally unknown or judged to be all of one type and at the lowest level of canines. No great intelligence is assigned to the many hundreds of thousands of dogs that were companions to the Indians. Except for the Eskimo Dog, romanticized by writers of fiction such as Jack London to be a special breed to be admired for sagacity and perseverence, all others are thought of as dumb beasts. Unfortunately, they were considered by the early white settlers to be good only for shooting and eating when desperately hungry.

Today there are no Indian dogs and all tribes except a few in the jungles of South America have been conquered, subjugated, and contained within the modern cultures that envelop their homelands. The true Indian cultures peaked in accomplishment and the development of Indian dogs peaked in extent just prior to the onslaught of the white man. With the arrival of Christopher Columbus and the subsequent wave on wave of followers from Europe, the great Indian population was gradually displaced and destroyed. The ravages of war swept away thousands. In North America, the killing continued from the first major battle at Pequot Fort, Massachusetts, in 1637 to the massacre of the Sioux band at Wounded Knee, South Dakota, in 1890. Just as the Indians were the casualties of warfare with the white man, so too were the dogs.

Whether shot by advance scouts of the attacking forces to silence the barking that alerted the Indians, or systematically exterminated after the massacre of a tribal group so that nothing of Indian life remained, the Indian dogs were under constant siege. They were hunted for sport, shot at for target practice, or driven into a feral state after the decimation of Indian owners. The ravage continued, from the first landings on the eastern coast of America to the shifting of the last remaining Indians to the western reservations. During the two hundred fifty year period of conflict between white man and Indians, movement of the white immigrants placed the recurrent battles ever westward.

73

During this same period, disease and pestilence swept forward to claim an even greater number of Indians. While superior fire power claimed a large portion of the male Indian population, epidemics of small pox, measles, typhoid, tuberculosis, dysentery, and other diseases wiped out whole tribes and decimated others. Slave merchants and fur traders, offering whiskey and other goods, encouraged activities that disrupted and, along with war and disease, eventually destroyed most Indian societies. This dismal period saw the American Indians sink to a pitiful level. Then tribes were banished to the reservations of the West.

Fortunately, in the last fifty years, there has been a gradual return to a more deserving status. There is an increasing popular awareness that Indians were, and are, kindred people like any other cultural group, and that included among them are the wise and foolish as well as craftsmen, leaders, dullards, statesmen, cowards, and heroes. Today there are close to one million North American Indians, with about half living on or close to reservations. There are college-trained Indians in all the professions and many have entered economic pursuits of the modern world. Nevertheless, the Indians of North and South America have resisted total assimilation and largely retain the values of their ancestors who once occupied the two continents.

Our view of the Indians and their dogs will be principally of circumstances during this early period, just prior to their encounters with the white man. Because of their tenaciousness in retaining older ways of life and thought, it is possible to learn about Indian dogs from the tribal activities on the reservations during the nineteenth century and early years of the twentieth century. These relatively modern factual accounts, along with the works of explorers, trappers, and artists, comprise rich sources for information about the Indian dogs of each cultural group.

Breeds of Indian Dogs

From the records of explorers, archeologists, and anthropologists, it can be stated conclusively that in the Western Hemisphere there were three main types of Indian dogs. They can be classified as (1) large wolf-like, (2) medium sized with erect ears but drooping tail, and (3) small, no larger than a Terrier. This latter type was either heavy of bone or slender in limb and skull. The first type clearly includes the large Eskimo Dog of the Arctic countries that is viewed typically as strong, powerfully built, with a broad muzzle, erect ears, and large bushy tail curled forward over the hip. The second is typically judged to be coyote-like, small in stature but with build, bone, and tail that resemble its wolf ancestor. The latter dog was seen most frequently among the tribes of the Plains and Southwestern Cultures and in Mesoamerica and South America. Of the third type, frequent references from the travelers of the late 1700s and early 1800s mention a "fox-like" dog among the Indians of both North and South America. These small dogs were noted as sometimes heavily built, sometimes with pointed nose and other times as short-nosed. Their considerable variation is a sign of crossbreeding to develop special features.

The main variable characteristics that are controlled by chromosomes form the basis for the identification of the various types and breeds. Dr. S. A. Asdell of Cornell University, in his book entitled *Dog Breeding: Reproduction and Genetics,* indicates the main characteristics to be as follows:

1—Body skeleton
2—Limb skeleton
3—Shape and set of head
4—Form of tail
5—Eye and skin pigmentation
6—Set of eyes and ears
7—Hair and color pattern of coat
8—Blood type
9—Behavior and hunting traits

The combinations and permutations of these various basic characteristics can account for all the differences seen today in domestic dogs, and surely they can be used advantageously to identify and compare the various dogs of the American Indians.

While it can be said that the American Indians had domestic dogs of three main types—a larger, a medium, and a smaller—there is ample evidence of numerous local breeds that are distributed among the cultural groups. Differences in coat, conformation, and manner are evident along with the general size—in height, length of body, or shape of skull. An intensive review of the records shows that seventeen distinctly different breeds can be identified, although it is likely that there were other breeds that could be classed along with the seventeen.

Even among some modern breeds that are recognized by The American Kennel Club, there are some with very similar characteristics. To the casual observer there is little, if any, difference between some breeds. Even the reasonably experienced fancier can be troubled to identify the Brittany and the Welsh Springer Spaniel, the Harrier and the Foxhound, and the Irish Water Spaniel and the Standard Poodle.

Early explorers or settlers, whose interest in Indians and their dogs was minimal, would be poor judges. Even to the careful observer there could be but little attention to minor differences in such useless objects as the dogs, when even the Indians were held in low regard. Differences would be ignored and breeds would go unrecognized under such circumstances.

Although the term "breed" is applied to the locally distinct forms of Indian dogs, it cannot be concluded that all were the result of a conscious effort to change or to keep constant the special features. Nevertheless, some circumstances indicate that this was indeed the process that produced the particular type. Dogs with a special coat and all of a type would certainly indicate a thoughtful breeding effort over a considerable time. The Klamath Indians of the Northwest Coast Cultural Group, who herded dogs on islands in the coastal waters of northwest Washington, were breeding consciously for the long white hair used for weaving. In other cases, a particular type of dog was so numerous and uncontrolled by the Indian owners that random breeding had to occur.

It is possible that individuals with favorite dogs of special color, size, disposition, or instinct singled-out their prized animals for special matings. Evidence of these controlled matings would not be observed in the mass of dogs that frequented the camps of some tribes of certain cultural groups. It was not uncommon for tribes to permit very large dog populations. There are references of some tribes of the Plains Indian Cultural Group that have ten to thirty dogs for each family. While there could be different types or even breeds among such canine throngs, it is very likely that only chance genetics controlled reproduction and the various types.

Although no single investigator can be credited with a systematic study of the aboriginal dog during the critical years prior to the general dispersal and destruction of the different Indian cultures, enough information is available to form a rather extensive picture. From a great variety of source material, much of the evidence was gathered by Glover M. Allen, and published in his seminal paper in 1920 while at the Museum of Comparative Zoology at Harvard College. The seventeen breeds identified from the prior record by Allen include all dogs in North and South America that are native to regions from the Arctic to Tierra del Fuego. The record also permits the identification of breeds that were included in each of the fourteen cultural areas.

Each cultural group of Indians is known to have had about three different breeds. Eastern Woodland Indians possessed the Common, Small, and Short-legged breeds, while the Southern South American

Indians had the Long-haired, Patagonian, and Fuegian breeds. The Sub-Arctic Group owned the Hare, Common, and Short-legged breeds, while the Northwest Coast Indians enjoyed the Klamath, Clallam, and Short-legged. Southeast Indians were known to have the Common, Small, and Short-nosed breeds. And the Mesoamerican had the latter two plus the Hairless. Arctic and Plains Indians had only two breeds: the Eskimo Dog and Malamute, and the Sioux and Plains, respectively. Two breeds were also found among the Great Basin, Plateau, and Caribbean Cultural Groups. Both of the first two groups owned the Plains and Common breeds while the last Cultural Group owned the Common and Hairless. Two cultural groups are known to possess four breeds. The Southwest Cultural Group owned the Plains, Small, Long-haired and Short-nosed dogs, while the Incas bred the Inca, Long-haired, Pug-nosed and Hairless. Only the Indians of California are credited with one breed—the Short-nosed dog.

It is apparent that certain breeds were more widespread than others and that some were found in only one cultural group. The Common Dog is aptly named since it is found in six cultural regions, which is more than any other breed. Three breeds, the Short-nosed, Plains, and Small, are found in four cultural areas, while three breeds, the Short-legged, Hairless, and Long-haired, are found in three cultural groups. All of the other ten breeds are found in only one Indian culture.

This distribution of the breeds indicates that selectivity prevailed in many instances. The fact that certain breeds are quite widespread indicates that a favorable condition encouraged growth of the breed. An abundance of food or the same need felt by many cultural groups could encourage common possession of a breed. Single breeds in cultures indicate special adaptation to local conditions and the fulfilling of a unique role. The descriptive material that is presented for each of the seventeen types of dogs of the American Indians will substantiate in many respects these general observations about the breeding patterns and purposes among the different cultural groups.

Above: Peigan Indian Camp with numerous Plains-Indian Dogs. This illustration by Bodmer was made in 1830 at the height of the horse/dog cultural period.

Below: Plains-Indian and Sioux Dogs as seen in a portion of the Rocky Mountain House painting by Paul Kane. (Royal Ontario Museum.)

78

Great Plains Dogs

Plains-Indian Dog

Distribution: Throughout the Great Plains Region in Western North American from British Columbia south, perhaps to the Mexican boundary.

Use: These medium sized dogs were used chiefly by the Indians as beasts of burden or to drag travois for transporting food, wood, clothing, and household goods. Also for hunting bear, running down deer, and corralling bison. They served as watchdogs and as food for symbolic or ritual purposes and during periods of famine.

General Appearance: Size medium, about 50 cm at the withers; ears large, erect; tail long, bushy, drooping or slightly curved; coat rather rough, usually pale yellow, brownish yellow, sometimes black and gray mixed with white; coyote shaped skull, typical occipitonasal length—170 mm, typical zygomatic width—105 mm; slender frame.

The earliest reference to the Plains-Indian Dog is given by Pedro de Castaneda in the *Journey of Coronado* written after the 1540 tour of exploration of the southwest. Francisco Vasquez de Coronado set out from Compostela, Mexico, with three hundred Spaniards and about a thousand Indians, and entered the region of Arizona and New Mexico. While portions of his party explored the Grand Canyon and the Hopi Indian culture, Coronado led an expedition east to Texas and northeast across what is now Oklahoma and Kansas. Although looking for treasure, he found only the ragged Wichita and Kansas Indians, the bison and the Plains-Indian Dog. While traveling through New Mexico, Castaneda wrote that "the people have dogs like those in this country, except that they are somewhat larger, and they load these dogs like beasts of burden, and make saddles, and they fasten them with leather thongs, and they make their backs sore on the withers like pack animals."

It is even recorded that Coronado followed the Indian practice and employed "dog-packing" in his travels into and out of the Great Plains of the Southwest. In Coronado's report of his encounter with Indians in

West Texas, he described how the Indians moved camp "with a lot of dogs which dragged their possessions. They travelled like the Arabs, with their tents and troops of dogs loaded with poles and having Moorish pack saddles with girths. When the load gets disarranged, the dogs howl, calling someone to fix them right."

A letter from one of Coronado's men, written in 1541, further describes the Plains-Indian Dog as a valuable aid.

"When they move, for these Indians are not settled in one place, since they travel wherever the cows (bison) move, to support themselves, these dogs carry their houses, and they have the sticks of their houses dragging along tied onto the pack saddles, besides the load which they carry on top, and the load may be, according to the dog, from 35 to 50 pounds."

These accounts show clearly the role of the dog as a pack-animal and are the first to describe the packing with tent poles used as a travois.

The second group of Europeans to see the Plains-Indian Dog were the Spanish explorers led by Espejo during his expedition through the southwest some forty years later. Espejo and his followers traveled into the wilderness north of Mexico to bring the Catholic faith to the Pueblo Indians. Encountering pack-carrying dogs, Espejo described them as "dogs which carry loads of two or three arrobas (40 to 65 pounds). They provide them with leather pack saddles, straps and cruppers. They tie them to one another like a pack train. They put fiber ropes on them for halters. They travel three to four leagues (10 to 12 miles) each day. They are medium sized shaggy dogs."

Dog packing was also common in the more northern territory of the Plains Indian. La Verendrye writes in 1738 of the Prairie Assiniboine of the Red River region in Manitoba, "they make the dogs even carry wood to make the fires, being often obliged to camp in the open prairie, from which the clumps of wood may be at a great distance.... The women and the dogs carry all the baggage." Even the Meriwether Lewis and William Clark expedition that was sent by President Jefferson in 1801 to explore "the Missouri Valley and the communication with the waters of the Pacific Ocean," reported Plains-Indian Dogs.

While in the home region of the Teton Dakota tribe, Sergeant Gass, head of the military contingent with Lewis and Clark, told of seeing dogs harnessed to "a kind of car" on which they transported their goods from camp to camp. He said that they could haul about seventy pounds. Naturally, the "car" was the travois. Some thirty years later George Catlin, painter and naturalist, who lived among the tribes of the Upper Missouri, observed that "Every one of them, who is large enough . . . is encumbered with car or sled . . . on which he patiently drags his load."

The many descriptions of dogs being used to carry, haul, or drag the possessions of the various tribes of the Great Plains, establish clearly this role for the Plains Indian Dog. So important was this use of the domesticated canine that in the thousands of years prior to the arrival of the horse, the welfare and survival of every Plains Indian family depended almost entirely upon their having a large number of dogs.

It was only during the early 1700s that the horse reached the southern plains. It took one hundred years for it to be dispersed widely and become important in the Plains-Indian culture. Even then, the horse only supplanted partially the role of the dog as the means of transport. The two aboriginal methods of using the dog for moving possessions were back-packing and pulling the travois, which was later adapted to the horse for larger and heavier loads. In the former method the load was either secured as a saddle on the dog's back or the weight was divided into two parts and secured in a sling on each side of the dog. This latter arrangement could be used advantageously to haul firewood or carry slabs of bison meat back to camp.

Fortunately, a great deal is known about the Plains Indians' treatment of dogs and the construction of packs and the travois. During the period from 1750 to 1900, numerous artists, naturalists, and anthropologists visited the tribes of the region west of the Mississippi and Missouri Rivers. Their records in prose and pictures contain a great amount of information about the Plains-Indian and Sioux Dogs that were common to this cultural group of tribes.

The artists Catlin, Bodmer, Kane, and Rindisbacher provide valuable pictorial evidence of the dogs and the methods of use for transport.

The work of Gilbert L. Wilson and Frank Gilbert Roe provide a wealth of factual information about these dogs and gather together most references from earlier writings. Wilson was able to live with a Hidatsa Indian family on the Fort Berthold Reservation for ten summers starting in 1908. Much of the information about Indian dogs of the Plains is derived from the Indian informants that Wilson questioned during his stays with the tribe. Particular information is provided by an old woman, Buffalo-Bird-Woman, who was born in 1840. Her narrative statements are an excellent source of facts that here can be only partially conveyed. A second informant, Wolf-Chief, born in 1849, related an account of a hunt made with dog and travois in 1866. The authenticity and completeness of these first-hand accounts result in an invaluable source of information about Plains-Indian Dogs and should be read in the original by students of Americana who seek a more complete picture.

The construction and dimensions of the travois did not vary greatly among the different tribes. As described by Buffalo-Bird-Woman, the two poles of the typical travois were joined over the dogs' shoulders to form an X or V. Although at times any type of wood was used, the Plains Indians preferred cottonwood or birch because of the lightness and flexibility. New poles were always kept on hand and the poles were cut green and peeled to remove the bark. They were dried thoroughly during the fall before being bound together to make a frame. The frame poles were about three to five centimeters in diameter with the thick end cut flat to act as a runner when resting on the ground. The best poles were curved slightly and bound together with the curve upward to form an arch between the dog and the ground. With the weight of the load bending the poles downward, the curved poles would be straight and the load would be carried high off the ground. If loaded excessively, the poles would be deformed or crack and would have to be replaced.

To join the frame, two poles were notched at the smaller ends and tied together with a piece of the tendon that holds up the head and neck of a deer or bison. The tendon was cut lengthwise into strips about one centimeter wide and immediately drawn around the poles three times and tied. When dried, they formed an iron-like band to hold the poles together. The poles would be replaced about every two years but the flat-woven basket that was tied between the poles would be used for many years.

After the woven basket hoop of ash was fastened at the four places where it crossed the poles of the frame, a skin saddle was joined to the closed ends to cushion the poles against the back of the dog. A skin folded with the fur outward was usual for this purpose. Rawhide thongs were fastened at the crossing of the poles to serve as a breast band and neck collar for the dog. Other thongs were tied to the basket for securing the load. The overall length of the assembly varied from three to five meters, depending upon the availability of poles and the size of the dog used to draw the travois.

Excellent examples of dog travois of the Assiniboine Indians are seen on page 70. This scene was painted originally in the field by Karl Bodmer, a Swiss artist who recorded Indian scenes for Alexander Philip Maximilian, Prince of Wied-Neuwied, during his 1833 trip to study the Indians of the upper Missouri. Bodmer's color artwork was reproduced as aquatint copper plate engravings. In a 1905 edition they appear as black-on-white etchings. The photographic reproduction on page 70 shows three dog travois propped together in the usual fashion when not in use. In the foreground, a typical Plains-Indian Dog is shown hitched to a short travois, which is being loaded by a squaw.

The importance of the dog to aid in transporting Plains-Indian baggage can be appreciated fully when it is realized that the tribes moved five to eight times during the year in search of the bison and new living space. During the late 1700s and early 1800s the Great Plains offered the most hospitable of living conditions for the various tribal groups. As can be seen in the illustration, also by Bodmer, which is reproduced on page 78, a Piegan Indian camp comprised over four hundred wigwams. It is clearly a pleasant grouping with a place for young and old to work and play with many horses and even a greater number of Plains-Indian Dogs. In the painting of the Piegan Camp there are more than thirty dogs, a small number indeed, since each wigwam usually had ten to twenty varying in size from young pups to old trail hardened packers and travois dogs. On page 87 the Teton Sioux of the Dakota region are shown on the move. This scene was painted by George Catlin during his trip to the Northwestern Plains in 1832. Catlin describes the break-up of camp, preparations for moving, and trail conditions in his *Letters and Notes of the Manners, Customs and Conditions of North American Indians* which he wrote upon his return to the East and which was published in 1842,

> . . . at the time announced, the lodge of the chief is seen flapping in the wind, a part of the poles having been taken out from under it; this is the signal, and in one minute, six hundred of them (on a level and beautiful prairie), which before had been strained tight and fixed, were seen waving and flapping in the wind, and in one minute more all were flat upon the ground. Their horses and dogs, of which they had a vast number, had all been secured upon the spot, in readiness; and each one was speedily loaded with the burthen allotted to it, and ready to fall into the grand procession . . . . Each one of these horses has a conductress, who sometimes walks before and leads it, with a tremendous pack upon her own back; and at others she sits astride of the horse's back behind her, clinging to her waist with one arm, while it affectionately embraces a sneaking dog-pup in the other.
>
> In this way five or six hundred wigwams, with all their furniture, may be drawn out for miles, creeping over the grass-covered plains of this country; and three times that number of men, on good horses, strolling along in front or on the flank; and, in some tribes, in the rear of this heterogeneous caravan, at least five times that number of dogs, which fall into the rank, and follow in the train and company of the women, and every cur of them, who is large enough, and not too cunning to be enslaved, is encumbered with a car or sled (or whatever it may be better called), on which he patiently drags his load—a part of

the household goods and furniture of the lodge to which he belongs. Two poles, about fifteen feet long, are placed upon the dog's shoulder, in the same manner as the lodge poles are attached to the horses, leaving the larger ends to drag upon the ground behind him; on which is placed a bundle or wallet which is allotted to him to carry, and with which he trots off amid the throng of dogs and squaws; faithfully and cheerfully dragging his load 'til night, and by the way loitering and occasionally

"Catching a little bits of fun and glee
That's played on dogs enslaved by dog that's free."

Some two years later in the Southern Plains, Catlin had the fortune to see the Commanche moving their wigwams and changing their encampment. This laughable, mixed-up scene, shown on page 85, is described by Catlin.

Several thousand were on the march, and furnishing one of those laughable scenes which daily happen, where so many dogs, and so many squaws, are travelling in such a confused mass; with so many conflicting interests, and so many local and individual rights to be pertinaciously claimed and protected. Each horse drags his load, and each dog, i.e., each dog that *will* do it (and there are many that will *not*), also dragging his wallet on a couple of poles; and each squaw with her load, and all together (notwithstanding their burthens) cherishing their pugnacious feelings, which often bring them into general conflict, commencing usually amongst the dogs, and sure to result in fisticuffs of the women; whilst the men, riding leisurely on the right or the left, take infinite pleasure in overlooking these desperate conflicts, at which they are sure to have a laugh, and in which, as sure never to lend a hand.

Winter brought new roles for the dogs of the Plains Indian Cultural Group. When settled in winter quarters and travel was limited by snow and freezing conditions, it was common for the tribes to venture out onto the prairie near their camp to hunt bison. Especially after deep snows, when rapid movement of the herds was limited, Indians on snowshoes, accompanied by their dogs, could get close. The scene on page 87 of Assiniboine Indians with their Plains-Indian Dogs is graphic evidence of this type of encounter.

The artist who painted this scene was Peter Rindisbacher, who, as a young immigrant from Switzerland, entered North America in 1830 by

Comanche of the Oklahoma Region on the march provide a laughable dog-fight scene for the brush of George Catlin during his 1834 visit to the Indian country of the Southern Plains.

way of Hudson Bay. Landing at Port Nelsen, he and the other family members journeyed overland to the south past Lake Winnipeg. They settled in the rich land surrounding the headwaters of the Red River near the present city of Winnipeg and south to Grand Forks. To the west, along what is now North Dakota, Saskatchewan, and Manitoba, dwelt the Assiniboine Plains Indians, about eight thousand in number. Pursuing bison with dogs and using drives to impound entire herds of bison were favored hunting methods of the Assiniboine and Cree.

Rindisbacher shows the dogs to be in fine form with full coat and bushy tail. We see at close quarters dogs with white muzzle, a light ruff, white furred legs, and dark body coat. The set of the ears and bushy tail are as described by other travelers among the Plains Indians. It is also evident that the Assiniboine Dogs shown by Rindisbacher are very similar to the dogs shown by Bodmer from the Piegan and Assiniboine tribes. It can be concluded that there was great uniformity in type, conformation, and overall appearance among the Plains-Indian Dogs of the northern and western tribes. The pictorial evidence shows that they were medium sized, active, and trainable for hunting and for use with the travois, pack, and sled.

Sioux Dog

Distribution: The North-Central Plains, principally across South and North Dakota and along the Upper Missouri River.

Use: Among the Dakota tribes for hunting, dragging the travois, or as a packer. Among the village tribes, for drawing the sled, as a packer, for hunting, as a guard dog, and for food during famine and for special ceremonies.

General Appearance: A large wolf-like dog, closely related to the Plains-Indian Dog but larger; typically gray rather than tawny in color; sometimes white, black, and black and white; also spotted; large erect ears, sometimes folded forward; usually a bushy scimitar-shaped tail carried out behind when moving, yet sometimes short tailed; medium length, smooth coat—about 70 cm at the withers for mature males— resembled the German Shepherd.

While there are many paintings that show the dogs of the Plains Indians and numerous firsthand accounts of the activities of the dogs and their appearance under a variety of conditions and locations, unfortunately, there is a total lack of any systematic study or

Above: Plains-Indian Dogs worrying bison on the Canadian Plains as they assist an Assiniboine hunter. By Rindisbacher, 1834. (United States Military Academy.)

Below: Western Teton Sioux on the move across the prairie south of the Teton River comprise a stream of horses and dogs more than five miles long. (By George Catlin, 1832.)

comprehensive statement about the dogs by any early investigator. During the fifty years of high-life on the Plains between 1780 and 1830, the total Indian population from the Comanche in the south to the Blackfoot in the north totaled about one hundred thousand.

Based on observations by Maximilian and Catlin of the total number of dogs that were reared by the typical Indian family of the Plains cultures, there must have been about two hundred thousand dogs in the Great Plains at the peak of development. Of this great number of dogs, about one-quarter were Sioux while the remainder were Plains-Indian Dogs. The Sioux Dogs were owned by the Dakota, Mandan, Hidatsa, and Arikara tribes. During this period, the Dakota tribes numbered about twenty-five thousand and had at least twice their number in Sioux Dogs. The nomadic Dakotas roamed freely over the South Dakota Plains while the other tribes that owned Sioux Dogs lived along the Missouri and practiced agriculture. Reports by Allen, Sir John Franklin, Catlin, and Prince Maximilian, all describe the Sioux Dog.

An excellent example of a Sioux Dog is the animal in the forward position in the painting completed by Bodmer in 1834 during the Maximilian expedition. The reproduction on page 89 shows two dogs dragging a toboggan of the Mandan Indians along the frozen Missouri, followed by others of the tribe hitched in a similar manner. Long thin poles joined together with rawhide form side traces that attach the dogs to the toboggan through fur-lined yokes around the neck of each dog. A special feature is the support strap laid across the back of the first dog to hold the wood traces at the height of the neck of the second dog. The trace then passes directly to the bottom of the toboggan. This arrangement permits both dogs to apply almost equal force to the trace and is similar to the straight all-leather hitch used by northern Alaskan tribes in attaching a line of Eskimo Dogs to a sled. The Sioux Dogs in the Bodmer etching show the behavior pattern of well-trained animals walking dutifully by the side of their master and straining to move the load along the ice. It is clear also that strong toes with good nails and pads were required to gain a firm hold on the slippery surface.

The year before the Bodmer sketch was made, George Catlin lived among the Mandan Indians in their mud-hut village on the Missouri River near Bismarck, North Dakota. During his visit to learn of their ways and to paint and sketch the many scenes, he found them to "live in a country well-stocked with buffaloes and wild horses, which furnish them an excellent and easy life; their atmosphere is pure, which produces good health and long life; and they are the most independent and the happiest races of Indians I have met."

Above: Sioux Dogs of the Mandan Indians hitched to a sled for winter travel. (Sketched by Karl Bodmer, 1834.)

Below: Mandan Indian Village, painted by George Catlin in 1833, shows a white Sioux-Indian Dog on a hand leash. (Smithsonian.)

The Catlin scene of a Mandan Indian Village, reproduced on page 89, shows these most gay and hospitable people enjoying the midday sun while they frolic and converse on and around the many spacious circular lodges. "Some are to be seen manufacturing shoes and dresses, and others, fatigued with amusements or occupations, have stretched their limbs to enjoy the luxury of sleep, whilst basking in the sun. With all this wild and varied medley of living beings are mixed their dogs, which seem to be so near to the Indians' heart, as almost to constitute a material link of his existence."

In this Mandan village scene, Catlin places one of the Sioux Dogs on a leash pulling its young owner across the open area of the village. We see a white Sioux Dog, in all ways typical of the breed. The fact that here is a white-coated dog should not be surprising when one considers that white-coated wolves were common on the prairie during this period. It is also known that some Indians were casual in arranging the matings of their dogs and occasionally permitted matings between wolves and dog bitches that were in heat. The appearance of these rather large wolf-like dogs in the Mandan and Dakota villages, with coats similar in coloration to the native wolves, indicates cross-breeding with white wolves.

The similarity in appearance is noted in a letter from Prince Maximilian to Hamilton Smith shortly after his famous expedition. The Prince likens the Sioux Dog to a wolf, "excepting that the tail is more curved, and the color is either absolutely grey like wolves, or white, black and black and white." In 1851, a frontier officer related in correspondence that "among the Sioux, the dogs are large and grey, resembling the Buffalo Wolf." There is ample evidence that these Sioux Dogs were a distinct breed of local origin and were consistently maintained by careful selection of pups from each litter. Buffalo-Bird-Woman, the Hidatsa born but ten years after the Catlin visit, explained:

Usually, there were from seven to ten puppies in a litter. As we wanted only big dogs, and those of the first litter never grew large, we always killed them, sparing not even one. From the second litter, we kept three or four of the puppies with large heads, wide faces, and big legs, for we knew they would be big dogs; the rest we killed.

In order that the mother might stay in good condition, we never saved more than three or four puppies out of any litter. When there were too many to nurse, the mother became poor in flesh, very often grew weak and sometimes died. Of the three or four puppies saved, we might choose one bitch and the rest males . . . .

90

As a puppy grew up he sometimes developed a surly disposition. He would bite and snap at people or fight with other dogs. Such a dog was killed. Sometimes the owner would kill him with the blow of a stick or he would ask some young man to shoot him with a gun or arrows. The carcass was taken down to the Missouri River and thrown over the bank . . . .

Male dogs were castrated to make them gentle and keep them fat. Uncastrated dogs were apt to be surly and would run away with other dogs that came around the lodge. A dog was castrated when about a year old; but if fat and in good condition, he might be castrated much earlier; but the year age was the rule.

We had but one breed of dogs in the village in old times, but the colors of the dogs varied greatly. Some of our dogs were pure black, some white, some blue, some red, and some spotted with every color. The majority of our dogs were spotted; there were only a few of one color. Some of our dogs were shaggy; some had short tails. A bitch might litter and have two puppies that would grow up with short tails about two and one-half inches long, while the rest of the litter might have bushy tails. Dogs with shaggy faces were apt to be mean and fight and be surly and cross.

All of our dogs were about the same size. Our old breed of dogs all had straight wide faces, heavy, but not short legs, and ears that stood erect like those of a coyote. The dogs were about the size of a wolf. Their hair was not very long and lay smooth and silky over the body. Our old Indian dogs had tails in general rather short and not so bushy as those I now see on the Reservation; and their tails curved upward somewhat at the end, not like a coyote's which lies straight.

This firsthand account of the Hidatsa Indian breeding program confirms practices that would ensure the development of a particular type of dog. There is additional firsthand evidence, though, that the breeding program was not entirely successful in eliminating surly and aggressive dogs from the breed. A. White and D. Thompson visited the Hidatsa in 1806, shortly after the Lewis and Clark Expedition, and reported:

We found it dangerous whilst in this village to stir out of the hut without a good stout cudgel to keep off the dogs; they were so numerous and savage as sometimes to defy the brandishing of our clubs, so that we were actually obliged to engage them. Therefore, it is necessary for a person to be constantly upon his guard against the equally troublesome children and dogs.

While moving among the lodges of a Hidatsa or Mandan village could be a frightful experience for a white man, life was secure and warm for the Indians, their horses and dogs, within the mud covered huts. The portion of the sketch by Bodmer (page 93) shows this typical gathering. The floors of the dwellings were of packed earth swept clean and polished by bare and moccasined feet. In the center, a skylight looms over the fire pit which was used for cooking and to dry skin clothing. These large huts, forty to sixty feet in diameter, contained walls and a roof of timber that was supported by a four pole and beam structure. Atop the wood roof was a fifteen centimeter layer of willow boughs and about a meter of earth and clay to form a waterproof shield.

Within the enclosure was space for about thirty people, with curtained beds arranged along the rear wall. Toward the front entrance were stalls for four to six horses and throughout were bed spots and areas occupied by the dogs. In the Bodmer sketch are two horses and two adult dogs. A bitch with two pups is in the foreground and a male and young one are near the chief at the center of the lodge. Young and old Indians are grouped around the fire to complete this peaceful scene of Mandan Indian domesticity.

The food of the Plains Indians usually consisted of berries, corn and herbs, and venison and buffalo. Feasts were prepared for friends and many pleasant and festive evenings were passed together. On very special occasions, to appease the offended spirits or to honor the presence of some important guest, the feasting included the flesh of that most prized and faithful animal, the dog. Catlin, in 1833, was a member of a party of Indian agents sent from Washington to visit the Teton Sioux, and an honored guest at such a feast. Catlin describes the special occasion:

> Some few days after the steamer had arrived, it was announced that a grand feast was to be given to the *great white chiefs*, who were visitors amongst them; and preparations were made accordingly for it. The two chiefs, Ha-wan-je-tah and Tchan-dee, of whom I have before spoken, brought their two tents together, forming the two into a semi-circle, enclosing a space sufficiently large to accommodate 150 men; and sat down with that number of the principal chiefs and warriors of the Sioux nation . . . .

An 1834 sketch by Karl Bodmer shows the life style of Mandan Indians and their dogs.

In the centre of the semi-circle was erected a flag-staff, on which was waving a white flag, and to which also was tied the calumet, both expressive of their friendly feelings towards us. Near the foot of the flag-staff were placed in a row on the ground, six or eight kettles, with iron covers on them, shutting them tight, in which were prepared the viands for our *voluptuous* feast. Near the kettles, and on the ground also, bottomside upwards, were a number of wooden bowls, in which the meat was to be served out . . . .

Catlin recorded this dramatic event, as shown on page 95:

In these positions things stood, and all sat, with thousands climbing and crowding around, for a peep at the grand pageant; when at length, Ha-wan-je-tah (the one horn), head chief of the nation, rose in front of the Indian agent, in a very handsome costume, and addressed him thus:

"My father, I hope you will have pity on us, we are very poor—we offer you to-day, not the best that we have got; for we have plenty of good buffalo hump and marrow—but we give you our hearts in this feast—we have killed our faithful dogs to feed you—and the Great Spirit will seal our friendship. I have no more to say."

Major Sanford then rose and made a short speech in reply, thanking him for the valuable present which he had made him, and for the very polite and impressive manner in which it had been done; and sent to the steamer for a quantity of tobacco and other presents, which were given to him in return . . . .

In this case the lids were raised from the kettles, which were all filled with dogs' meat alone. It being well-cooked, and made into a sort of a stew, sent forth a very savoury and pleasing smell, promising to be an acceptable and palatable food. Each of us civilized guests had a large wooden bowl placed before us, with a huge quantity of dogs' flesh floating in a profusion of soup, or rich gravy, with a large spoon resting in the dish, made of the buffalo's horn. In this most difficult and painful dilemma we sat; all of us knowing the solemnity and good feeling in which it was given, and the absolute necessity of falling to, and devouring a little of it. We all tasted it a few times, and resigned our dishes, which were quite willingly taken, and passed around with others, to every part of the group, who all ate heartily of the *delicious*

Sioux Indians and United States commissioners at a feast. The pots contain a stew of the favorite dogs of the chiefs as an offering of great sincerity. This painting by George Catlin was completed in 1833 while he was living with the Sioux Indians.

viands, which were soon dipped out of the kettles, and entirely devoured; after which each one arose as he felt disposed, and walked off without uttering a word. In this way the feast ended, and all retired silently, and gradually, until the ground was left vacant to the charge of the waiters or officers, who seemed to have charge of it during the whole occasion.

This feast was unquestionably given to us, as the most undoubted evidence that they could give us of their friendship; and we, who knew the spirit and feeling in which it was given, could not but treat it respectfully, and receive it as a very high and marked compliment.

As one reads this description of a solemn incident in the lives of these generous people, one is filled with a mixture of remorse, repugnance, and respect—remorse for the faithful Sioux Dogs that were sacrificed for the occasion, repugnance toward the thought of eating the strange dog flesh, and respect for the Indian chieftains who had the strength and generosity to give their most valued possessions. As Catlin eloquently states, such acts of selflessness were marvelous examples of a generous spirit common among the Plains Indians:

Since I witnessed it on this occasion, I have been honoured with numerous entertainments of the kind amongst the other tribes, which I have visited towards the sources of the Missouri, and all conducted in the same solemn and impressive manner; from which I feel authorized to pronounce the *dog-feast* a truly religious ceremony, wherein the poor Indian sees fit to sacrifice his faithful companion to bear testimony to the sacredness of his vows of friendship, and invite his friend to partake of its flesh, to remind him forcibly of the reality of the sacrifice, and the solemnity of his professions.

The dog, amongst all Indian tribes, is more esteemed and more valued than amongst any part of the civilized world; the Indian who has more time to devote to his company, and whose untutored mind more nearly assimilates to that of his faithful servant, keeps him closer company, and draws him nearer to his heart; they hunt together, and are equal sharers in the chase—their bed is one; and on the rocks, and on their coats of arms they carve his image as the symbol of fidelity. Yet, with all of these he will end his affection with this faithful follower, and with tears in his eyes, offer him as a sacrifice to seal the pledge he has made to other men; because a feast of venison, or of buffalo meat, is what is due to every one who enters an Indian's wigwam; and of course, conveys but a passive or neutral evidence, that generally goes for nothing.

I have sat at many of these feasts, and never could but appreciate the moral and solemnity of them. I have seen the master take from the bowl the head of his victim, and descant on its former affection and fidelity with tears in his eyes. And I have seen guests at the same time by the side of me, jesting and sneering at the poor Indian's folly and stupidity; and I have said in my heart, that they never deserved a name so good or so honourable as that of the poor animal whose bones they were picking.

For a final view of the Plains-Indian and Sioux Dogs, the Canadian artist Paul Kane has recorded in color a gathering before the Fort at Rocky Mountain House. Completed about 1840, the painting reproduced on page 78 shows white, gray, and brownish-red coated dogs resting in the sun while Indian women construct summer shelters of tree brush. The white Sioux Dog is similar to the one in the watercolor by Catlin (page 89) that shows the leashed animal dragging the young Indian boy. The smaller gray dog is a Plains-Indian Dog similar to the coyote, while the two larger dogs of reddish-brown coat are typical of the Sioux Dogs described by Buffalo-Bird-Woman. These latter dogs confirm the description for this larger of the Indian dogs of the Great Plains.

Above: Portion of the earliest drawing of Eskimos with a dog, which appeared in the 1578 French edition of Dionyse Settle's account of the Frobisher voyages.

Below: Iglulik Indians at Winter Island north of Hudson Bay on Arctic Circle, as seen in sketch made in 1822 by George F. Lyon during Parry Expedition. When in the village, Eskimos leashed or tied the foreleg of dogs to prevent straying.

Arctic Dogs

Eskimo Dog

Distribution: Originally found in Arctic America among the coastal Eskimo tribes from Greenland to northwest Alaska. In the East it was probably no further south than Smith Sound, Greenland, and Northern Labrador; in the West, no further south than the Aleutian Islands.

Use: In winter, for sled work, usually in a sprayed hitch and as a draft animal; in summer as a pack animal. As a hunter, to track, corral, and attack polar bears; to seek and find the blow holes of seals in snow covered ice. For food, during periods of famine, to feed first the other dogs, and lastly to be eaten by the Eskimo family. As guide-dogs, to aid the return of lost parties, although at times unreliable. For clothing, hide sewed into leggings that were worn fur side in.

General Appearance: Strong; appearing like a wolf, but with straight-forward looking eyes, shorter muzzle, and higher forehead; tail curved sharply forward over the hip; coat thick, with short under-fur overlaid with longer hair up to 20 cm long at the shoulders; tail bushy with long hair; color of coat—whitish with dusky or dark blanket on the back varying to black, black and white, or tan and white; height to withers—50 cm; length, occiput to root of tail—70 cm; occiput to end of nose—28 cm.

Of the four modern northern dogs, namely, the Eskimo, the Siberian Husky, the Samoyed, and the Alaskan Malamute, the Eskimo Dog is most frequently confused for one of the others. While in fact a most famous aid to Arctic explorers, it seldom is credited with the special exploits that we have come to associate with sled dogs of the Far North. Yet it is truly "the dog of the Eskimo tribes." It was first recognized by Europeans who discovered Greenland and Baffin Island in the late 1500s. Subsequent contacts with the tribes to the west, across the Arctic Circle and continuing through to the early years of this century, always showed the Eskimo Dog to be a vital part of the existence patterns of these people of the Far North. From the first landing at York Sound by

Master Martin Frobisher in 1577 to the dash to the North Pole by Admiral Robert E. Peary in 1909, the Eskimo Dog has been a subject of great interest. Because of the essential services that he has provided in the Arctic, he continues to survive and prosper while most of the other aboriginal dogs were abandoned and disappeared. Even today the Eskimo Dog is maintained in the more remote towns in the Arctic, far up in the Northwest Territories of Canada.

From the descriptions of early writers, we can make reasonable comparisons with present-day animals and find a continuing presence of the same type of dog. Although his role as sled dog is now greatly diminished by the use of the gasoline-powered snowmobile, he still is needed for seal and polar bear hunting and is maintained as pet and companion by many who value his ancient heritage.

The earliest record of Eskimo Dogs appears in the 1582 text of Richard Hakluyt's *Dive Voyage Touching the Discoverie of America*. Here Hakluyt presents material from Dionyse Settle, a gentleman adventurer who accompanied Martin Frobisher. Settle relates exploits of a landing party from the Frobisher ship that encountered deserted tents of Eskimos near York Sound and "not taking anything of theirs except one dogge." The dogs are described as "like unto woolves, but for the most part black, with other trifles, more to be wondered at for their strangeness, than for any other commodities needefull for our use." Also, in the Hakluyt work, Frobisher reported, "they frank or keepe certaine dogs not much unlike wolves, which they yoke together, as we do oxen & horses, to a sled or traile: and so carry their necessaries over the yee and snow from place to place: as the captive, whom we have, made perfect signes. And when those dogs are not apt for the same use: or when with hunger they are constrained for lacke of other victuals, they eate them: so that they are as needfull for them in respect of their bignesse, as our oxen are for us."

Settle relates how a captive Eskimo at Frobisher Bay, at the southeast tip of Baffin Island, used an Englishman's dog to show the native method of training animals to haul sleds. "Taking in his hand one of those countrey bridles, he caught one of our dogges and hampred him handsomely therein, as we doe our horses, and with a whip in his hand, he taught the dogge to drawe in a sled as we doe horses in a coach, setting himselfe thereupon like a guide: so that we might see they use dogges for that purpose that we do our horses. They drawe with dogges in sleads upon the yee, and remoove their tents therewithall wherein they dwell in Sommer."

The earliest sketch of an Eskimo Dog appears in a 1578 French edition of the account of the Frobisher voyage written by Settle. A portion of the woodcut sketch probably based on an original painting by John White is shown on page 98. This primitive scene shows Eskimos hunting with bow and arrow and an Eskimo dog hitched to a sled with a shoulder harness. Such a strange Arctic scene must have been indeed wondrous to the English and French at that time. The sketch identifies clearly at this early date the role of the Eskimo Dog as a vital beast of burden among the Indians of the Far North.

In the same period, John Davis encountered Eskimo Dogs in Cumberland Sound during his search for the Northwest Passage. As related by Hakluyt, Davis "heard dogs houle on the shoare, which we thought had bene volves, and therefore went on shoare to kill them. When we came on land the dogges came presently to our boat very gently, yet we thought they came to pray upon us, and therefore we shot at them, and killed two: and about the necke of one of them we found a leatherne coller, whereupon we thought them to be tame dogs."

More than two hundred years would pass before the next account would be written about fauna of the Arctic. In 1829, John Richardson reported on the zoology of the northern parts of British America in his book, *Fauna Boreali-Americana*. As chief zoologist on Captain Sir John Franklin's Expedition to Northwest Canada, Richardson described the "Borealis Esquimunx Dog" encountered during the trip from Great Bear Lake down the Mackenzie River to Aklavik and the Beaufort Sea. Richardson describes the Eskimo Dog as follows:

The dog has short conical ears like the American wolf but its nose is still shorter than that of the latter animal. Its nose, cheeks, belly and legs are white. The forelegs are destitute of the black marks above the wrist which characterized the European wolf, and which is visible too in some American wolves. The top of the head and the back are almost black but there is a narrow white line down the spine of the back. Its sides are thinly covered with long black and some white hairs and there is a shorter dense coat of yellowish grey wool. The tail like the back is clothed with black and white hairs. Dimensions: Length from the end of the nose to tail—4'3", length of tail—1'2", height of the ears—3", breadth between the eyes—2½", breadth between the ears —4½".

Just a few years before Richardson described the Eskimo Dog after his return from the Franklin Expedition, George F. Lyon, who commanded the ship Hecla, wintered over in 1822 with the Iglulik Eskimos. Lyon got along well with the local Indians and recorded his experience in 1824.

The scene on page 98, which appeared in Lyon's book, shows the Eskimo village at Winter Island. Eskimo Dogs with the typical coiled tail are abundant. They are shown either leashed or with foreleg tied to prevent straying. Lyon sketched the sleds of the Iglulik Eskimos as long and flat with cross pieces to form a ladder construction.

On page 103, Polar Eskimos are shown a thousand miles further north with sleds that have a back rest and are laced together with leather thongs. This portion of a painting by the Eskimo John Sackhouse appeared in the book by John Ross about his 1818 expedition to find a sea lane to the Orient across Arctic America. While the sleds are quite different, we know that the team was hitched in the usual fan arrangement. This is shown very well in the Sackhouse painting where the sleds are tied by individual leather bindings to groups of four or five dogs.

In Greenland and Canada, the dog sleds most often looked like ladders and the teams were hitched in a fan-shaped arrangement with traces about two meters long. Three to eight Eskimo Dogs pulled a sled and were guided by the Eskimo driver. A long thong whip, five to eight meters in length, was used, along with "shouts," to direct the team by flicking the whip end precisely at an ear or flank of a laggard. Each thong of the fan-hitch was usually equal although at times the lead dog was on a longer trace.

When stopped, the driver would wedge a front paw of each dog in its harness to prevent the team from running off with the sled. The traces were fastened between the harness of the dog and a thong loop at the front of the sled. With this arrangement, each dog could pick its own trail over the rough ice. Also, the risk of breaking through ice was considerably lessened as the weight of the team was distributed widely over about a three to five square meter area. The dogs could also break the rush of a sled while descending a grade by spreading out to right and left as far as possible. At times they could even be hitched to the rear of the sled to manage the descent of very steep grades.

The central-trace hitching pattern was used in northwestern Alaska. The dogs were staggered on either side of a single strong leather thong. This arrangement is required in countries where there are trees along the trail since the fan-shaped hitch would be impossible to manage in wooded areas. The northern-Alaskan sled was also different from the flat ladder sled used in eastern and central Canada. The bed of the sled was high and fixed to stanchions that rested on the rails. At the rear were high stanchions that could be used to guide the sled and to hold during travel. The rear stanchion could be pulled backward to retard movement,

Portion of painting by John Sackhouse made in 1818 of members of Ross Expedition meeting Polar Eskimos near Thule, Greenland. The fan-hitch for a team of dogs was common among Canadian and Greenland Eskimos.

pushed forward to aid travel or pushed laterally to break the runner free if frozen fast. The design of the sled accommodated the deep and sometimes wet snow encountered in western Alaska.

The Northwestern Eskimos used a five or six dog team and could travel about ninety kilometers a day when conditions were good.

Further to the west among the Yuk-speaking Eskimos of the Unaligmiut and Kwikpagmiut tribes, Russian Lieutenant Lavrentiy A. Zagoskin reported in 1842 that the dogs were "harnessed to the stanchions" of a sled and that "the art of travel with dogs is in its infancy; they have no lead dogs, no trained teams, and they never sit on their sleds." Dogs were harnessed to the stanchions at the sides of the sled and the Eskimos pushed the sled from behind and pulled with lines at the front. This old method of hitching dogs is well documented. It was judged inferior by Zagoskin—undoubtedly because of his experience with dog teams hitched in the usual fashion by the Siberian Eskimos. Just as there was ample reason to use the fan-hitch and the central-trace arrangements, the side-hitch offered advantages to the far western Eskimos in managing sleds in the particularly deep snow conditions of their coastal locality.

Some interesting observations about the training and hauling ability of dogs of the Central and Eastern Canadian Eskimos are given in *The Private Journal of G. F. Lyon*, published in 1824:

Having now possessed during my second winter a team of 11 very fine animals, I was enabled to become better acquainted with their good qualities than could possibly have been the case by the casual visits of the Eskimos to the ships. The form of the Eskimo dog is very similar to that of our Shepards dogs in England but he is more muscular and broad chested owing to the constant and severe work to which he is brought up. His ears are pointed and the aspect of the head is somewhat savage. In size a fine dog is about the height of the New Foundland breed but broad like a mastiff in every part except the nose. The hair of the coat is in Summer as well as in Winter very long but during the cold season a soft downy undercover is found. Young dogs are put into the harness as soon as they can walk and being tied up for so long soon acquire a habit of pulling in their attempts to recover their liberty. When about 2 months old they are put into the sled with a grown dog and sometimes 8 or 10 little ones are under the charge of some steady older animal where with frequent and sometimes cruel beatings they soon receive a competent education. Every dog is distinguished by a particular name and the angry repetition of it has an effect as instantaneous as the application of the whip which instrument is of an immense length having a lash of from 18 to 24 feet while the handle is only one foot. At one time 7 of my dogs ran a mile in four minutes drawing a heavy sled full of men. Afterward in carrying stores to our ship "Fury," one mile distant, 9 dogs drew 1600 lbs in the space of 9 minutes.

Lyon says in another passage,

Eleven dogs were large and even majestic looking animals and an old one of particular sagacity was placed at their head by having a longer trace so as to lead them through the safest and dryest places. These animals having such a severe dread of water as to receive a severe beating before they would swim a foot. The leader was instant in obeying the voice of the driver who never beat but repeatedly called him by name. When the dogs slackened their pace, the sight of a seal or bird was sufficient to put them instantly to their full speed. It was a beautiful sight to observe the two sledges racing at full speed to the same object, the dogs and men in full cry and the vehicles splashing through the holes of water with a velocity and spirit of rival stagecoaches. The Eskimo dogs are likewise useful to their masters discovering by the scent the winter retreats which the bears make under the snow.

Some ten years later, in 1840, John James Audubon prepared the first American painting of the Eskimo Dog for his book, *The Quadrupeds of North America*, with text by Reverend John Bachman. Writing about the "Esquimaux Dog," Bachman used Richardson as his main source of information while Audubon used the descriptive statements as the basis for his painting of the dog. The dog shown on page 106, the Audubon Eskimo Dog, appears to be heavy-coated and more refined than the photograph of the Coppermine Eskimo Dog taken by Vilhjalmur Stefansson in 1908 and shown on page 107. The group of Eskimo Dogs shown on page 108 accompanied the Robert E. Peary Expedition to the North Pole. The dogs were gathered from Eskimo villages along the coast of Greenland and Baffin Island during the 1907-8 winter. They represent but a few of the 133 that were on board ship with Peary for the long cruise up Baffin Bay to the Lincoln Sea in the Arctic northwest of Greenland. These Eskimo Dogs are larger than the original dogs that aided the Arctic Indians prior to the arrival of the white explorer. Studies of measurements from nine skulls of old Eskimo Dogs from Greenland,

The Eskimo Dog as drawn by John James Audubon in 1840 was found across the Arctic Coast from the west coast of Alaska to Greenland and south to Labrador and Newfoundland.

Typical dog of Coppermine Eskimos who lived along Coronation Gulf in the central region of the Canadian Northwest Territories, two hundred miles north of the Arctic Circle. (Photograph by Vilhjalmur Stefansson, 1908.)

107

A few of the Eskimo Dogs that pulled nineteen sledges for Robert E. Peary, six Expedition members, and seventeen Eskimos in the month-long dash to the North Pole in 1909. The final run was made in the last five days by Peary, Matthew Henson, and three Eskimos. (Peary.)

Baffin Island, Labrador, Mackenzie, Alaska, and eastern Siberia show them to be about the same size as the Common Indian Dog. The measurements show them to be smaller than the present Eskimo Dog which has been influenced by crossbreeding with larger European types during the past 150 years.

The best size Eskimo Dog has been a constant issue of discussion between Eskimo natives and European explorers. Vilhjalmur Stefansson, the explorer, noted in his book, *The Friendly Arctic*, that, "For one thing, the Eskimo dog is too small. Those we have had ran in weight from fifty to seventy pounds, and to haul such a load as our six dogs were carrying would need at least nine of the best Eskimo dogs. The disadvantage of having nine dogs as against six is plain. There is the trouble of harnessing three more in the morning and of unharnessing, tying and feeding them in the evening. True, a bigger dog needs a little more food, but six dogs weighing 120 pounds each will do well on less food than is necessary for nine dogs averaging 70 pounds."

Stefansson is comparing the working ability of purebred Eskimo Dogs with Saint Bernards and Mastiffs crossbred with wolves and Eskimo Dogs. He is obviously concerned with the logistics of Arctic travel by Europeans with heavy loads, little time, and less patience. For regular use over long periods, even Stefansson agrees that, "The Eskimo dog has one advantage in the soundness of his feet, and another in his good fur. Certain kinds of white men's dogs have even better fur, but I know none that have feet as sound, or at least as little affected by adverse polar conditions. It is in this soundness of the feet that half Eskimo blood gives the chief advantage above the pure bred Saint Bernard, whose fur also needs improvement."

Although the Eskimo Dogs were a vital aid in the movement of families to new homes and in the carrying of Eskimos by sled while they searched for seal, caribou, and bear, it was as hunting dogs that they showed their true worth. For most of the year the dogs of the Canadian Eskimos were used primarily for hunting and only secondarily as shaft animals. During the long winter, fishing or whaling was not possible. Only hunting for game over the ice and snow would provide food and skins needed for the survival of each Eskimo, his wife, his children, and even his dogs.

Over the frozen sea near shore, seals were caught through small holes in the ice made from below by the seals for breathing. In the same snow-covered ice fields, the polar bear was speared by two or three hunters together after the bear was attacked and held by their dogs. On frozen tundra, at favored locations on caribou trails, Eskimo hunters would wait with their dogs to attack, drag down, and kill young caribou bulls or females from the edge of the herd. After a kill, whether bear, caribou, or seal, dogs were used to drag, carry, or haul the fresh carcass back to camp. There, with help from other family members and friends, the bloody work was completed, to provide meat, blubber, bone, skin, and fur. All helpers would receive tasty morsels, including the dogs who would sleep with full stomachs as their special reward.

To find seals beneath the vast expanse of level ice far at sea required a special partnership of man and dog. The breathing holes are occasionally visible on an area of ice swept clean of snow by the wind, but since the seal does not like the light when breathing, the cleared holes usually are abandoned by the seals. The ones in use are invisible since they are covered with a layer of snow. The breathing holes are about three centimeters in diameter and cannot be found without the aid of a good scenting dog. As Vilhjalmur Stefansson reports after spending many years among the Canadian and Greenland Eskimos shortly after 1900,

If you believe that seals are found here and there all over the polar ocean, you will infer when a dog wants to pause and sniff the snow that a seal's breathing hole is concealed underneath. This inference is usually right, for there are few other things up there that smell.

If you allow it, the dogs may begin to dig in the snow as a dog would for a rodent. You must not permit it, for daylight in the breathing hole will scare the seal. The dogs' usefulness is over when they have scented out the holes. You lead or drive them to a distance of a few score yards where they lie down and sleep.

In seal hunting by this method of spearing the game through a hole, it is advisable to have a number of hunters since in each area there may be a number of breathing holes. When one hole is located, other hunters take the dogs on a leash and lead them around in circles until as many holes are located as there are hunters. The method depends entirely on the ability of the Eskimo Dog to detect the faint traces of seal breath left in the snow above the small hole during the previous breathing period. Consider also that the air temperature is usually well below freezing, -20 to -40 degrees Centigrade, and a wind is usually blowing across the surface of the snow. The scenting prowess of the Eskimo Dog must be truly great.

While the dogs must be skilled in finding seal holes, the Eskimo must be both agile and extremely patient to spear the quarry. After inserting a small ivory rod that resembles a coarse knitting needle into the hole so that the lower end will be nudged upward by the nose of the seal as it rises to breathe in the hole, the Eskimo must stand motionless above the hole, waiting hours or even days. Since the seal cannot be seen or heard, the slight movement of the rod is the only signal to strike through the hole with the harpoon. The long wait for the seal to rise is necessary because there may be a dozen other breathing holes scattered over several acres of snow-covered ice and used alternately by the seal. At the right instant, if the harpoon hits the small hole, it will also hit the nose of the seal just below. Harpooned and held by a line, the hole is enlarged with an ice chisel, permitting withdrawal of the seal onto the snow. Now another role for the dog is at hand. As observed many times by Stefansson and reported in his book, "The Friendly Arctic," the Eskimo, ". . . hitches the dog to (the seal) and sends him home to camp. The dog does this errand with the greatest good will for he knows that he is going to get a feed at the end of it. I have asked Eskimos whether the dog was not likely to stop on the way to eat the seal, but it seems that this rarely or never happens. Before the dog starts he may try to lick the blood off the seal but he will not stop even for this when once on his way. However, if the seal is caught by a snag of ice and the dog gets stuck, he may turn on the seal and eat it. When a dog once learns to eat a seal on the way home it is difficult or impossible to break him of the habit and thereafter such a dog is never entrusted with a seal."

From the start to finish of this "mauttok" or waiting method of seal hunting, the Eskimo Dog plays critical roles: first by locating the many breathing holes; then by waiting patiently and quietly near by, comforting the waiting Eskimo by his presence during his long wait; lastly, by dragging the dead seal back to camp. In this final role, the Eskimo Dog pulls across the snow and ice a load weighing typically seventy to ninety kilograms or about four times his own weight. The haul could be over rough or smooth surfaces and a distance of more than a mile from the Eskimo village. While the scenting ability was no doubt acquired as a result of selective breeding, the unattended hauling over long distances was the result of extended training by the Eskimo master. Both actions show an animal performing with considerable intelligence.

A more natural response of Eskimo Dogs occurs with the scent of polar bear. When a bear trail either is crossed during sledding or is seen at a distance, the dogs know that bear meat is near and send up a great howl. The Eskimo method of bear hunting starts with the release of the dogs so that they can dash forward and surround the game. As described by Stefansson, "Commonly two or three Eskimos hunt bears together, although any Eskimo would be ashamed of not tackling a bear alone if no hunting companion happened to be available. It is considered that two or three dogs should be used although some exceptionally good bear dogs are able to hold a bear singly. . . . There is a scramble and uproar and excitement. The dogs bark while unhurt and howl with pain if the bear gets a blow at one of them that does not disembowel or otherwise kill him instantly. . . . The bow and arrow are occasionally used, especially if there are several hunters, but more often the bear is killed with the hunting knife converted into a spear, for these Eskimos have no regular spears."

Certainly polar bear hunting is a far more dangerous sport than seal hunting and requires entirely different dog behavior. This is shown vividly in the scene by Parry which is reproduced on page 113.

The search for food was continuous and required travel for long periods of time by dog teams. The maintenance of a good team was as important as a man's skill with weapons. Only in times of extreme need, when dying of hunger was the only alternative, were the dogs killed for food. Since they too had to be fed, the number kept by the Eskimo was neatly balanced. It could not be more than could be fed properly from the resources from the hunt, nor less than can drag a sled over long distances in extreme winter weather. A typical team was from four to six dogs while a large team consisted of seven dogs.

Because of their importance, it was essential that considerable care be expended in the dogs' behalf. The bitch with a litter was kept in the tunnel to the snow house, or a small house was built nearby for whelping and raising the litter. While nursing pups, the bitch's teats were protected from freezing with a piece of skin tied beneath her body. In spring, boots were used to protect the dogs' feet from sharp ice crystals. The pups were playthings for the Eskimo children. They had free run of the village until they were old enough to be trained for the harness.

To make a small puppy grow quickly, odd practices were followed. To get a large dog it was considered necessary to pull the head, legs, and body of the small pup. Even more perplexing, air was blown into its anus! Also, an amulet was tied around the neck of a puppy in order to help it mature quickly into a useful animal. This latter practice may have been used to accustom the pup quickly to the collar and harness that it would soon wear as a worker. When a young dog was added to a team it was given a name to be used to teach it to obey commands. Loud and frequent shouts of the name accompanied the lash of the long whip to make a willing dog. Encouraged and punished in turn, the young novice soon learned to be a help to the team mates. Since great skill was required to use the whip, children began to learn the skill at an early age and spent most free time each day practicing with small whips on puppy teams. The

Eskimo attitude toward dogs was a mixture of concern and cruelty. While dogs were whipped with abandon and often underfed, they also were considered as members of the family. When food was scarce, they starved with the people; when abundant, all ate well. Dogs were recognized as the vital element in the welfare of the Eskimo. It was absolutely critical to have a good team for hunting and for moving the family to a more favored place in the continuing search for food.

So great was the bond between the Eskimo and his dog that almost everywhere across the Arctic, dogs were considered to have supernatural powers. The most widespread myth associated human origin with the mating of a dog and an Eskimo woman. So strong was the need for the dog, that his survival was assured, even in the face of crossbreeding with European dogs of various breeds.

It is estimated that prior to the arrival of explorers during the first half of the nineteenth century, the Eskimo population distributed from Greenland to Alaska was about fifty thousand and that this number was maintained until the early 1900s. Considering the size of dog teams and Eskimo families, it is reasonable to assume that the Eskimo dog population fluctuated around one hundred thousand animals. With this number of the breed and selection by owners for matings with the more intelligent and hardy lead dogs, the uniformity of type that was observed by so many of the early European visitors would be maintained. In fact, there are still some authentic examples of this grand dog today in the Far North along the Arctic Circle in Canada.

As shown in this illustration made during the 1822 Parry Expedition to find the Northwest Passage, Eskimo Dogs frequently were tossed and killed when they attacked a polar bear.

Above: The Hare-Indian Dog was bred and trained for hunting by the Indians north of the Great Lakes and west to the Rockies. (Audubon.)

Below: The Hare-Indian Dog as sketched in 1836 by John Richards during his study of the zoology of the Northwestern MacKenzie District, Canada.

Sub-Arctic Dogs

Malamute

Distribution: Northwestern Alaska along the shores of Kotzebue Sound and into the interior along the Kobuk River drainage basin occupied by the Kovagmiut, Selawikmiut, and Malemiut Eskimos, all of the Inuit Cultural Group.

Use: Principally for sled hauling; as a hunter, to track and corral polar bears and to find breathing holes of seal in snow covered ice; for food during famine; and as a guide-dog during blizzard conditions.

Appearance: Large (60 to 80 pounds), strong with deep chest and compact body; head broad; ears erect and pointed; height to withers, 60 cm; heavily boned; coat thick, with short underfur overlaid with longer hair; tail bushy with long hair curved over the hips; color of coat usually light gray and ranging through black with white on underbody, legs, and feet.

All the various descriptions in the previous section about the Eskimo Dog apply also to the Alaskan Malamute—except for one significant feature. What distinguishes the Malamute from the other three famous sled-dogs—the Siberian Husky, the Samoyed, and the Eskimo Dog—is size. Ranging to twenty pounds heavier, three inches taller at the withers, and having the heaviest bone, the Malamute is considered the giant of sled-dogs of the North Country.

While there is considerable early historical evidence in prose and pictures to confirm the appearance of the native Eskimo Dog, it was not until the early part of this century that the Malamute was identified as an Arctic sled-dog. There is little in the historical record prior to 1900 to place a large version of the Eskimo Dog in northwestern Alaska, although in any group there are always individual dogs of larger size. It is accepted that the Malamute, officially recognized today by the Canadian and American Kennel Clubs as a distinct breed, is a modern version of the original. As a result of selective breeding beginning around 1925, the general appearance has been altered and shaped to suit the fancy of the modern owners of this hardy animal.

Actual measurement of skulls as a basis for comparison between dogs from across the Arctic was made by Allen in 1918. He reported that of nine skulls of Eskimo dogs collected during the mid-1800s from Greenland, Baffin Island, Labrador, Mackenzie, Alaska, eastern Siberia, and Kamchatka, "most are of about the size of those of the Common Indian Dog." He also reported that those from Siberia were the smallest while the largest skull of the group was from Nulato, Alaska, along the Yukon River. It would have been fortunate if this skull had come from the Kotzebue Sound or Kobuk River area since this is considered the original home of the Malamute Dog. The very name Malamute is a corruption of the Eskimo tribal name, Malemiut, which in turn means, "people of the Male area." This tribe and the Kovagmiut and Selawikmiut lived along the coast of Kotzebue Sound and the Kobuk River just north of the Arctic Circle on the western side of Alaska. Although Allen notes the large size of the Alaskan skull, he states that, "This and other large skulls of Eskimo Dogs, probably are the result of crossings with large dogs of European origin. It seems apparent that the large size of some stock, and that probably the aboriginal Eskimo Dog was not a much larger animal than the Common Indian Dog. The thick coat, however, often adds much to its apparent size."

Considering that selective breeding of the Malamute by the white man began just a few years before the Allen study, it is reasonable to assume that the Malamute stock already had been altered by crossbreeding at even earlier times.

The first documented visit to the Eskimos of Kotzebue Sound and the Kobu River region, other than by traders and whalers, was by the crew of the Revenue Cutter Corwin in 1880. By 1883, Navy and Revenue Marine officers from the Corwin were engaged in explorations. Led by Captain Michael A. Healy, Naval Officer George M. Stoney, and Lieutenant Jon C. Cantwell, the Kobuk River was surveyed during two summers and the nearby Eskimo tribes were studied.

The Kobuk Eskimos had abandoned long ago sea-mammal hunting along the treeless coasts to live inland along the banks of the Kobuk River. Recent archeological studies show continuous occupation dating back for at least a thousand years. Their summer quarters were tents of bark slabs and moss rather than skins, while the winter houses were of logs, snow covered, and entered through a tunnel.

This region experiences deep and powdery snowfalls, so the local tribes had to devise special arrangements. For instance, snowshoes provided winter mobility. Only in this region were snowshoes so important, because the snow cover over the other Eskimo lands across the Arctic is usually much less deep or is crusted by the wind. A second unique aspect was the design of the dog sled and the hitching arrangement. To pass through deep snow the sleds used along the Kobuk had a built-up bed and stanchions topped with rails. They were also of lighter construction than similar sleds further north and east. The bed, set high off the runners, could pass over the deep snow more easily and the stanchions could be used by the Eskimo driver to help push the load. Because a track in deep snow is necessary for the dogs, it was not unusual for the wife of an Eskimo to break trail ahead of the team. Also to aid movement in deep snow, all the dogs of a team were hitched to a single long trace. This arrangement also aided movement in single file through timbered areas to avoid obstacles that would catch dogs that were in a fan-hitch.

The deep snow also would make a bigger dog desirable. The typical Eskimo Dog of medium build would flounder in the snow along the Kobuk. It would be natural for the Malemiut Eskimos and the neighboring tribes to select gradually only the larger, longer limbed Eskimo dogs for breeding. Through a process of adaptation to environmental conditions, the Eskimos of the Kobuk region could have solved their problem of winter transport. It is reported by Captain Healy that a five-dog team could cover about forty kilometers in a day under the usual conditions of the trail. The report of the Healy expedition also includes ample description of dogs of the Malemiut Eskimos.

They had dogs of. . . beauty and endurance. The dogs travel hundreds of miles and are better cared for by their drivers than is the usual lot of Arctic dogs. The dogs are powerful looking, have thick dense double coats (outer coats of thick coarse fur and inner coat a fuzzy down lying close to skin) called weather coats, erect ears, magnificent bushy tails carried over their backs like waving plumes, tough feet, colors varying but mostly wolf gray or black and white. The dogs have remarkable endurance and fortitude. The Malemiut people and their dogs are much respected among other Inuits.

Although it cannot be said with certainty that the Malemiut Eskimos possessed a different breed of dog than the many other Eskimo tribes in Alaska, Canada, and Greenland, it is reasonable to identify their dogs as a distinct type among the varieties owned by the American Indians. No

117

doubt as Alaska was opened to traders and gold seekers, there was intermingling of blood between the native Eskimo Dogs and those brought in from the lower United States. Larger, powerful dogs were prized as team members to haul enough supplies for a year into the back country. Crossbreeding under such circumstances would be a natural condition. The Malemiut teams of today, capable of hauling sleds loaded to a thousand pounds, are clearly the ancestors of the leading Eskimo dogs of the north.

Hare-Indian Dog

Distribution:　In the Northwest Territories of Western Canada around Great Bear Lake, southwest to Lake Winnipeg and Lake Superior and west to the Mackenzie River. Named after the Hare Indians but owned also by the Bear, Mountain, Dogrib, Cree, Slave, and Chippewa Tribes.

Use: In the chase over snow for game such as rabbit and deer; as a regular source of meat among certain tribes; to make fur coverings for winter wear; as a beast of burden to haul a small travois, pack, sled, or toboggan.

Description: A small dog, slightly larger than a fox but smaller than a coyote; rather slender proportions; small head with sharp muzzle; erect thick ears; somewhat oblique eyes; rather slender legs and broad hairy feet; bushy tail with long hair; face, muzzle, and legs white, larger patches of dark blackish gray or lead color over back; ears white in front, tail white beneath and at the tip; affectionate disposition.

The Hare-Indian Dog was named by John Richardson in his 1829 report of observations made during participation in the Captain Sir John Franklin Expedition to Northwest Canada. The Franklin party entered North America by way of the Saint Lawrence River and the Great Lakes. From there they traveled overland in a northwest direction to Great Slave Lake, Great Bear Lake, and the Mackenzie River. They finally boated down the Mackenzie to the Arctic Sea. The Franklin party was the first to explore this region. Along the way Richardson had ample time to meet and study many people from the north Canadian Indian tribes. He spent considerable time observing the Mackenzie Eskimos. In his writings, Richardson gave the Hare-Indian Dog an equal amount of attention as the "Esquimaux Dog." So taken was Richardson by this friendly little animal that he purchased for company a puppy from the Hare Indians. In his report, Richardson states:

118

The young puppy which I purchased from the Hare Indians became greatly attached to me and, when about seven months old, ran on the snow by the side of my sledge for 900 miles without suffering from fatigue. During this march frequently, of its own accord, it carried a small twig or one of my mittens for a mile or two. Although very gentle in its manners, it showed little aptitude in learning any of the arts which many Newfoundland dogs so speedily acquire of fetching and carrying when ordered. This dog was killed and eaten by an Indian on the Saskatchewan (River) who pretended that he mistook it for a fox.

Richardson noted that the Hare Dog was very playful, had an affectionate disposition, and was soon friendly when treated kindly or offered bits of food. It was very fond of being caressed, and rubbed its back against the hand like a cat. It made friends quickly with strangers. Nonetheless, the Hare-Indian Dog was not docile, nor did it tolerate punishment or confinement of any kind. Richardson observed that it would dart away if rebuked and "if it was conscious of having deserved punishment it would hover around the tent of its master the whole day without coming within reach when called." It was a very speedy little dog and could outrun and dodge the larger mongrel dogs at Fort Franklin, on the Mackenzie River, where the exploring party stayed for some time.

The dash and sprinting ability of the Hare-Indian Dog may have been the primary reason for the development of this breed. Before firearms were obtained by the northern Indian tribes, a dog of light weight and speed would be invaluable in the open country for running down small game. Additionally, Richardson reports that this type of dog had rather wide paws, or so it appeared because of the long hairs that projected from between the toes. He noted that it could pass rapidly over the snow in pursuit of game in the winter. He stated that the Hare-Indian Dog was spread generally amongst the Indian tribes north of Lake Winnipeg where similar winter ground cover conditions prevailed and the use of such a dog would be advantageous and a common need.

A painting of the Hare-Indian Dog was completed by John W. Audubon in 1849 and is shown on page 114. It is based on the sketch by Richardson shown on the same page, his description, and a stuffed specimen from the London Zoological Society. The dog appears rather larger than the one that can be imagined from the Richardson description and sketch and somewhat out of proportion, with a body too heavy for the size of the head. A more likely view of the Hare-Indian Dog appears in Peter Rindisbacher's paintings of the various modes of travel of the Chippewyan Indians. These paintings, now at the West Point Military

Academy Museum, were made about the same time as the Richardson reports were written. At the lower left corner of the upper illustration on page 121, is a good likeness of the dog described by Richardson, but hitched to a small travois. The lower illustration on page 121 shows two dogs in a straight hitch dragging a toboggan. The dogs in these pictures by Rindisbacher almost fit exactly the descriptions by Richardson of height, shape of head, ears, tail, and feet. While the coat color is as described for the tail, legs, and body, the solid colored blankets are different from the patchy coat in the Audubon picture and Richardson's sketch. Of course, the artist may have been partial to solid coats, just as some breeders are today with dogs that normally have patchy coats. Since the Chippewa Indians were identified by Richardson as having the Hare-Indian Dog, and Rindisbacher painted in the area of Canada occupied by the Chippewa, we can accept these, along with the Richardson sketch, as authentic pictorial examples of this breed. A true comparison can be made by referring to the pictures and the following statement about the breed by Richardson in his 1829 report.

The Hare-Indian Dog has a mild countenance with at times an expression of demureness. It has a small head, slender muzzle, erect thickish ears, somewhat oblique eyes, rather slender legs and a broad hairy foot with a bushy tail which usually carried curled outward. It is covered with long hair particularly around the shoulders and at the roots of the hair, both on the body and tail, there is a thick wool. The hair on the top of the head is long and on the posterior part of the cheek it is not only long but being also directed backwards, it gives the animal when the fur is in prime order the appearance of having a ruff around the neck. Its face, muzzle, belly and legs are of pure white color and there is a white central line passing over the crown of the head and the occiput. The anterior surface of the ear is white, the posterior yellow, grey or fawn color. The end of the nose, the eyelashes, the roof of the mouth and part of the gums are black. There is a dark patch over the eye. On the back and sides there are larger patches of dark blackish/grey or lead color mixed with fawn color and white not definite in form but running into each other. The tail is bushy white beneath and at the tip. The feet are covered with hair which almost conceals the claws. Some long hairs between the toes project over the soles but there are naked callous protuberances at the root of the toes and on the soles. Its howl when hurt or afraid is that of the wolf but when it sees any unusual object it makes a singular attempt at barking commencing by a kind of growl, which is not however, unpleasant and

Above, Chippewa Indians' mode of travel with their dogs in spring and summer. By Rindisbacher. (United States Military Academy.)

Below: Chippewa Indians' mode of travel with their dogs in winter. By Rindisbacher. The dogs illustrated here and above correspond with John Richardson's 1829 description of Hare-Indian Dogs. (United States Military Academy.)

A portion of the painting "A View of the River LaPuce near Quebec," by Thomas Davies, 1782. Dogs with white coats were prized by the Indians for sacrificial purposes, and for the coat itself for use as a robe.

ending in a prolonged howl. Its voice is very much like that of the prairie wolf.

We know from the statement by Richardson that his Hare-Indian Dog was eaten by a Chippewa Indian. It is also known that the Chippewyan tribe used dogs to supplement the diet during periods of hunger. These tribes are thought to have emigrated from the eastern part of Canada. Their legend is that they once migrated from the Atlantic Coast, north of the Saint Lawrence, guided by a magic shell. This tale would indicate that the Hare-Indian Dog came along during the migration and existed among the northern tribes of East Canada at much earlier times.

It is reported in the account of Frobisher's voyage to eastern Canada in 1577 that the expedition found in addition to large dogs used for sledding, a smaller breed that apparently was used only as food, and that was allowed the freedom of the Indian's tents. Hakluyt reports that the historian of the expedition stated that they "found since by experience, that the lesser sort of dogges they feede fatte, and keepe them as domesticall cattell in their tents for their eating, and the greater sort serve for the use of drawing of their sleds."

The same writer relates that, at York Sound, on going ashore to examine "certaine tents of the countrey people," they "found the people departed, as it should seeme, for feare of their comming. But amongst sundry strange things which in these tents they found, there was rawe and new killed flesh of unknowen sorts, with dead carcasses and bones of dogs."

Allen, in his paper on the dogs of the American Indians, when writing about the small dogs found by Frobisher at York Sound, concludes, "They may have been a dwarf variety of the Eskimo dog, or as seems likely, a small breed similar to those of the Hare Indians or of other tribes of the mainland." What is known, of course, is that two hundred years after the Frobisher visit, a small, friendly Hare-Indian Dog was identified clearly in words and pictures as a numerous possession of the tribes of Middle Canada.

Above: An Ojibwa Indian on snowshoes, with his family and dog-drawn toboggan near Lake Winnipeg. Color lithograph by W. Day after H. Jones, ca. 1820. (Archives of the Legislative Buildings, Victoria, B.C.)

Below: A representative of the Short-legged Indian Dog breed owned by the Bersimis Indians of Quebec, Canada. (Photograph by W. P. Cabot, ca. 1910.)

124

Northwest Coast Dogs

Short-legged Indian Dog

Distribution: Eastern Canada, New England, south to New York. In the Far West from British Columbia, south to Northern California. Wherever canoe-using and forest tribes lived.

Use: As a household pet for the children and women; as a scavenger to rid the campsite of bones and spoilable refuse; as a hunting companion for the men and to keep them warm at night when sleeping in the open; to hunt small game such as beaver, ground hog, and other burrowing animals.

Appearance: Large head for size of body; erect ears; long body compared to height; broad breast and heavy hindquarters; legs relatively short and straight, not distorted; sleek fur of medium length, white, or spotted liver and white; tail upturned with longish hair; overall appearance like a Basset Hound but with straight legs and longer hair.

This breed of dog was described by early travelers among the Indians in the Northeast and explorers of the Far West. Evidence for its existence is found also in archeological excavations along the New England Coast. The shell-heaps of Frenchman's Bay, Maine, that were excavated by F. F. Loomis and D. B. Young in the early 1900s were a rich source of dog bones. Portions of the skeletons and teeth of more than sixty individual dogs were uncovered. Loomis and Young reported their work in *The American Journal of Science* in 1912 and described fifteen specimens of Eskimo Dog, thirty specimens of the Common Indian Dog, and fifteen of the Short-legged Indian Dog. Allen had the opportunity to study and measure these specimens. He was able to identify clear differences between the latter two types of dogs. The Short-legged Indian Dog has smaller size teeth as well as a shorter row of teeth compared to the Common Indian Dog. The teeth of the smaller dogs are more close-set and, as is usual in American aboriginal dogs generally, the first premolars of both the upper and the lower jaw are usually missing. The typical leg

125

bone of the Short-legged Indian Dog is about three-quarters the length of those of the Common Indian Dog. The humerus and the radius measure about 130 mm while the femur is proportionately longer, about 136 mm. The length of these limb bones indicate a dog about the height of a Basset Hound.

The first to describe the Short-legged Indian Dog was John Richardson after his return from the exploration of northwestern Canada. Writing in 1829, he related that a friend gave him a present of an excellent example of the Short-legged dog of the Attnah or Carrier Indians of British Columbia, Canada. He intended to bring the dog to England. He related that, unfortunately, "it was stolen and fell a sacrifice to the desire which a party of Canadian voyagers had to partake of a meal of dog's flesh." Richardson stated, "I regretted the loss the more as intending to have a portrait taken of it I neglected to draw up a detailed account of its characteristic features."

Nevertheless, Richardson remembered enough about the general appearance to prepare the following description:

It had erect ears and a head large in proportion even when compared with the Eskimo Dog; its body was long and its legs short; its fur was rather shorter and sleeker than that of the other native dogs and its body was studded with small spots of various colors. There was a good deal of intelligence in its countenance mixed with wildness. It was extremely active and could leap to a great height. Carrier Indians used it in the chase. It was of the size of a large Turnspit Dog, and had somewhat of the same form of body but it had straight legs and its ears gave it a different physiognomy.

While reported by Richardson among the Carrier Indians, the Short-legged Indian Dog was also found in 1860 by members of the transcontinental railroad survey party near Eel River, in the interior of northern California. George Suckley in his report described "one peculiar looking dog . . . among very wild Indians. It had short legs and long body, like a turnspit." In the same report, Suckley also noted:

The Indian dogs about the Dalles of the Columbia (River) are so varied that no special description can be given. We might, however, make out two types. The large . . . and the small, resembling the "turnspit kind." The latter are generally white, or spotted liver and white, or black and white. This kind is kept more as a playmate for the children and a pet for the women.

126

It is obvious from the accounts of Richardson and Suckley that a dog, similar to the Turnspit Dog with spotted coat, lived among the Indians of the Canadian Rockies and Northern Cascade Mountains up to the late 1800s. In these heavily wooded regions, canoes were the usual means for travel and a small dog would be carried easily. Similar conditions prevailed for the Indians of the northeast. One of the last persons to pay particular attention to dogs of the Indians in the northeast states was S. T. Livermore. In his *History of Block Island* he describes the Short-legged Indian Dog as still present on this isolated outpost in 1875. The record shows that the Manissean Indians on Block Island numbered about fifty by 1800 and entirely disappeared by 1885. Livermore was familiar with the last of the Indians and their Short-legged Dogs. In 1877 he wrote:

The "dogs" of Block Island belonging to the Manisseans before the English came have their descendants here still, it is believed. They are not numerous, but peculiar, differing materially from the species which we have noticed on the mainland, both in figure and disposition. They are below a medium size, with short legs but powerful broad breasts, heavy quarters, massive head unlike the bulldog, the terrier, the hound, the mastiff but resembling mostly the last; with a fierce disposition that in some, makes but little distinction between friend and foe.

While there are no etchings or paintings of the Short-legged Indian Dog, we do have artistically prepared sketches and a description of the Turnspit Dog of the late 1700s. In both Britain and the American Colonies, this short-legged and stocky animal was laboring to turn the mechanical contraptions that rotated the sides of meat over the open hearth fires of many a home.

Dr. Abraham Rees described briefly the Turnspit Dog in his *Universal Dictionary of Arts, Science and Literature* that was published in Philadelphia in 1806. His section on "The Dog in Zoology" was the first book about dogs available in America. Of course, much of the information had its source in British dog books. Nevertheless, the work was a significant addition to the body of knowledge about zoology and dogs for the young Americans. Rees described the Turnspit Dog as follows:

A spirited, active and industrious kind of dog, considered once as an indispensable attendant of the spit, which, by a peculiar contrivance,

127

and the aid of its own exertions, it was enabled to turn at an even pace. This office of the canine turnspit has, however, been gradually superseded by the introduction of the "jack" in this country, except in some particular places. It is still practised in France and Germany. The turnspit is distinguished by having the body long, the legs very short, and the tail curled on the back; its usual colour is greyish with black spots. There are three varieties of this family of dogs, one of which has the feet straight, another the feet curved, and the third having the body covered with long curly hair.

The archeological evidence studied by Allen, and the descriptions by Richardson, Suckley, and Livermore all support the existence of the Short-legged Indian Dog that was a match with the Turnspit Dog. They apparently were the familiar household pet of the Indians that lived in the heavy forests of the northeast and northwest coastal regions. A dog photographed about 1900 by William P. Cabot is shown in the lower illustration on page 124. It was a dog owned by the Bersimis Indians of Eastern Canada and was judged by Allen as being representative of the Short-legged Indian Dog. It has many of the characteristics that were identified by the earlier explorers and naturalists. The small size of this animal would make it a favorite as a companion during travel by canoe.

It is reported that the Short-legged Indian Dog was especially adept at beaver hunting. A Jesuit, Le Juene, in 1633 described how Indians of the Quebec region hunted beaver with "petit chien . . . that pursue and take it easily." Another visitor of the Indians noted "The dogs which were small enough to enter this hole (of the beaver)." Yet another use for this small heavy-set animal is gleaned from the tales of travelers among the Indians and the bone remains in the archeological digs. In time of hunger or for ritual purposes during burials, the Short-legged Indian Dog was killed for food, or to serve as a guide for its loving owner for safe passage to the world after death.

Larger or Common Indian Dog

Distribution: Found among the forest Indians from eastern Alaska southeastward to Newfoundland and Florida and the Greater Antilles, and westward from the Atlantic Coast to the edge of the plains in the east central states. Also in the Great Basin and Plateau region of the western United States.

Use: For food during feasting and periods of famine; as a hunter, singly and in packs to corral game such as deer, moose, bear, lynx, and small rodents; in the North to haul sleds and toboggans; in the South as a pack animal.

Appearance: Long-limbed, slightly smaller than the Greyhound; skull rather slender with high forehead and a knife-like sagittal crest; wolf-like in appearance with slender frame and a small rear; ears large, sharp-pointed, and erect; coat rough, wooly in the North to silky or satiny in the South; color of coat uniform black or white to marked blackish and white, or reddish brown; northern dogs a little larger than those in the South; zygomatic width—102 mm, alveolus to occipital condyle—175 mm, humerus—164 mm, radius—164 mm, femur—170 mm, tibia—170 mm; first premolar usually missing.

Gonzalo Fernandez de Oviedo, a Spanish navigator and explorer, reported the extended journeys of his countrymen in his *General and Natural History of the Indies* published in 1535. In this work he writes about the Common Indian Dog of the Caribbean. He had observed the dogs in the Island of Haiti shortly after the discovery, although he declared that they were all gone by 1535, that during a time of famine, all had been killed for food. He describes the Common Dog as of all colors, some uniform and others with blackish and white or bay colored markings. He noted that coats were rough with somewhat longish hair of smooth texture. The ears were pointed and erect like those of wolves.

Dog was accepted fare among the Caribbean Indians, and Oviedo and other Spanish explorers ate it often. Oviedo described it as an excellent meat somewhat like lamb. He noted that the Indians bred numbers of dogs and at their great festivals considered the high point of the occasion the serving of great dishes of dog-meat. The dogs usually were "split along the spine and roasted on one side." While good to eat, the dog also was used by the natives to hunt other meat, especially the nutria, a rat-like rodent with a body about forty centimeters long. For eating, the nutria was considered the next best thing to dog!

While Oviedo was the first to write about the Common Indian Dog, Christopher Columbus had been the first important European to see one. It was late in the afternoon on October 17, 1492. The previous day, Columbus had left the Islands of Santa Maria de Concepcion in the Bahamas sailing west and came upon "a very wonderful harbor" at the northwest end of Fernandina Long Island. He went ashore with some of his men and a few natives that he had picked up at previous stops. After a short walk inland to investigate, he reported in his journal "and there were dogs, mastiffs and terriers." While we cannot doubt that Columbus saw dogs, we can certainly question his description of the animals. More likely he saw the Common Indian Dog which he called "mastiffs," and the Hairless Dog, which he described as the "terrier." A week later he wrote in his journal of stops along the north coast of a nearby island and "in one of them he found a dog that didn't bark." This was at Bahia Boviary, Cuba, six miles from the present town of Puerta Gebara.

The entries Columbus made in his journal during this first visit to the West Indies were commented upon by Bartolome de Las Casas some fifty years later. Las Casas was a missionary among the Caribbean Indians from 1502 to 1520 and had ample opportunity to observe the native dogs. He wrote in his *Historia de las Indias* that Columbus must not have seen the dogs personally but repeated sailors' reports, "... for if he had seen them he would not have called them masties, for they look like podencos (hounds); these and the small ones never bark, but only have a sort of grunt in the throat and are like the dogs of Spain, only differing in that they don't bark."

At another time Las Casas called one of the dogs "Gozcos," because he thought it resembled just the plain "cur" dog of his Spanish Peninsula homeland. On the other hand, "Podenco" Espagnol, the oldest of the Spanish Hounds that have been bred for centuries in Spain, was surely well known to Las Casas. There can be little doubt that he was referring to the Larger Common Indian Dog when he made the comparison. The Podenco Espagnol of today is a rare remnant of its older cousins, yet still retains an original appearance. This medium-sized dog with narrow skull, erect and pointed ears, slender, long limbs, and satiny coat matches well the composite descriptions of the Common Indian Dog.

How widespread over North America was this Larger Indian Dog can be judged by another description that appears in Hakluyt's *Voyages*. It appears in the 1593 account of the voyage of the ship Marigold when stopping along the coast of Cape Breton Island, Nova Scotia. The historian relates the events of an accidental meeting between some of the ship's company and a party of "Savages." Upon the discharge of a musket, the Cape Breton Indians came "running right up over the bushes with great agilitie and swiftness . . . with white staves in their hands like halfe pikes, and their dogges of colour blacke not so bigge as a greyhound followed them at their heeles; . . . but wee retired unto our boate."

An observer of wolf and dog in the middle states in the pre-Revolutionary period informed John Hunter that the dog found in the country of the Cherokee Indians was "very similar to the wolf with erect ears." While B. S. Barton, writing in 1757, recalled seeing, when a boy,

Indian Dogs accompanying their owners on visits to his father's farm in Pennsylvania. He later described the dogs as having a "body, in general more slender than that of our dogs. He is remarkably small behind. His ears do not hang like those of our dogs, but stand erect, and are large and sharp-pointed. He has a long, small snout, and very sharp nose."

Barton also said that during the late 1700s this type of dog was still maintained by careful breeding among the Indian tribes of the Six Nations. Barton considered this fact worth noting because by this period in most other regions along the eastern seaboard, the few remaining Indian dogs were fully crossed with a variety of European breeds. Of some significance, therefore, is the painting by Thomas Davies that was completed in 1782 of a Larger Indian Dog. A portion of the painting, entitled "A View of the River LaPuce near Quebec," is reproduced on page 122. The dog matches quite well the descriptions noted earlier, including pointed ears, longish face, light limbs, wolf-like overall appearance. Even the solid white longish coat is judged to be an acceptable northern variation.

Although the Common Indian Dog was a source of food among most of the tribes of the Sub-Arctic, Eastern Woodland, Southeast and Caribbean Cultural Groups, it also was a vital partner in the hunt for game. This relationship was observed by many of the explorers and early settlers of the Eastern Seaboard region.

One of the first English sea captains to investigate the Maine shores reported in his log of the 1604 voyage that "he saw eighty-three Indians near Pemaguid Point in a Hunting party. Everyone of them was with his bowe and arrowes and with their dogges and wolves."

Just a few years later, "five or six people with a dog" were spotted by a shore party of the Plymouth settlers. As reported in *Mourt's Relation,* the journal of the Pilgrims, on December 15, 1620, they were set ashore on the northwest side of Cape Cod. There, "when they ordered themselves in the order of a single file and marched about the space of a mile, . . . coming towards them, were savages, who when they saw them ran into the wood and whistled the dog after them."

The details of an Indian hunt with the Common Dog are told by Nicholas Denys, who lived in the Gaspe Region during the middle of the seventeenth century. He reported:

When they took their Dogs to hunt the Moose in spring, summer, and autumn, the Dogs would run about for some time, some in one direction and some in another. The one which first met some track followed it without giving tongue. If he overtook the beast, he got in front of it, jumping for the nose. Then he howled. The Moose amused himself, and whisked to kick the Dog in front. All the other Dogs which heard it came running up and attacked it from all sides. It defended itself with its feet in front; the Dogs tried to seize its nose or ears. In the meantime the Indian arrives, and tries without being seen to approach within shot below the wind. For if the animal perceives him or his smell, the Moose takes to flight and scorns the dogs, unless the hunter gives it an arrow-shot. Being injured, it has difficulty in saving itself from the Dogs, which followed it incessantly, as does also the Indian, who overtakes it and shoots again. But sometimes the Dogs, which have seized the ears or the muzzle, drag it to earth before the Indian has come up. They are not inclined to abandon it, for very often they have had nothing to eat for seven to eight days. The Indian arrives, completes the kill, splits open the belly, and gives all the entrails to his Dogs, which have a great junket. It is this which makes the Dogs keen in the chase. . . .

In hunting lynxes with dogs, Denys said that "This animal mounts into a tree where it is easily killed, whilst the Dogs are terrifying it with their barkings. All the other animals are not really difficult to kill, and there is not one of them capable of attacking a man, at least unless it be attacked first."

For beaver, the Common Indian Dog was used as a scenting hound. Denys reported, "For (hunting) of the Beavers, it also was done in winter with Dogs, but they were only used to find the houses in which they smelled the Beavers through the ice."

As the land became occupied by settlers from Europe and the Indian tribes traded their forests for the new objects of value offered by the land-hungry immigrants, the hunting range gradually diminished. It was inevitable that there would be conflicts and acts of trespass for the Indian and his dog. One case that shows the full scope of the problem involved Ben Uncas, the chief of the federation of Algonkian Tribes of the North Atlantic states. In October 1715, Ben Uncas petitioned the local legislature that he and his son had been "ignorant" of a recently passed law which they had violated.

Shortly before, a law had been passed that forbade "for better Preservation and Increase of Deer" killing at "unseasonable times" or from the middle of January until July. The son of Uncas, "a Young Lad . . . encouraged there to by examples of the English . . ." had killed the previous winter with "his dog" a number of deer. The boy was charged with the complaint, seized and brought by a special unit before William

Pitkin, Esquire. He was fined a sizable sum, five pounds! The evidence brought against the boy shows conclusively that the Mohegan Indians hunted deer with their Common Dogs.

The fine was paid by Uncas, otherwise his son would have been sold into slavery, yet he could hardly afford the penalty. So great was the hardship of the fine that Uncas petitioned the legislature. He opined that the sum was "very grievous" to him and would "greatly impoverish" his family. He promised to conform to the law if the fine was returned to him. He promised to refrain from hunting "unless pinching necessitie" and hunger did "force him upon violation thereof." Alas, the humbling statements of the exalted chief were rejected by the House, although accepted by the State Senate. The money was not returned. A few years later Ben Uncas with his family and dogs moved west from Connecticut into the Mohawk Valley. There he found freedom once again to hunt the deer in the forests of his native America.

And when the hunt was over and the chief and his braves were well fed, the Common Indian Dog filled another role. In addition to their aid in the hunt, dogs were welcome as sleeping companions. In most teepees and lodges, the warmth of the dog served to dispel the cold of the night. The Jesuit Missionary Le Jeune, who lived with the Huron and Montagnais, spent many a night with both Indians and the dogs. Writing in 1634, he described a sleepless night with Indian Dogs in a Montagnais' home: "These poor beasts, not being able to live outdoors, come and lay down sometimes upon my shoulders, sometimes upon my feet, and as I only had one blanket to serve both as covering and mattress, I was not sorry for this protection, willingly restoring to them a part of the heat which I drew from them. It is true that, as they were large and numerous, they occasionally crowded and annoyed me so much, that in giving me a little heat they robbed me of my sleep, so that I very often drove them away."

Such warmth, so needed under primitive conditions, was but one of the acts of companionship provided to many an Indian by a favored dog. Le Jeune noted in his reports that among the Huron, dogs "are held as dear as the children of the house, and share the beds, plates and food of their masters." An instance, motivated no doubt by the same feelings, was reported to Le Jeune. The instance demonstrated recognition of love and affection for a dog. For the burial of a young Indian girl, the parents requested the Jesuits to prepare a large grave because they wished to bury her belongings with her. When they arrived for the ceremony, they had among the possessions her two dogs. The parents asked permission "to bury them for the dead girl loved them" and they wished to give to the dead girl "what she loved" when she was alive. Le Jeune also reports that the request was denied!

Besides many tales about the Common Indian Dog, there have been numerous archeological finds of the skeletal remains of this companion to the Indians. In the course of explorations in Florida and Georgia, many remains have been unearthed. Also identified as remains of Large Indian Dogs are three crania from Madisonville, Ohio; two from La Moine, Maine; fragmentary skulls from Cuba; a skull from Peel River, Yukon; three complete skeletons at Stratford, Connecticut; and a skeleton at Port Washington, Long Island. These remains and the descriptions of the dog contained in so many of the early writings confirm fully the presence of the Common Indian Dog over the vast area of North and Eastern America.

Small Indian Dog

Distribution: Found among the forest Indians of the Northeast and Southeast Cultures along the Atlantic Seaboard. Also found across the region bordering the Gulf of Mexico, in the central and southwestern part of North America, and parts of northwestern South America.

Use: Principally for food, although also, when puppies, as playthings for the young children; special males and brood bitches held as companions for the women and men; sometimes for the hunting of small game.

Appearance: A small, slender-limbed dog; narrow, delicate head with fine muzzle; ears erect and pointed; a longish, slightly curved, close-haired tail; color of coat black, black and white, or brownish yellowish; fox-like overall, with sharp nose.

Francisco Hernandez, writing in 1578, was the first European to describe the Small Indian Dog. He knew it to be found in Mexico and called it the Techichi. He noted that it was raised by the Indians principally for eating, had a melancholy visage, similar to a spaniel, but was otherwise like a small Common Indian Dog. He added that it was one of three types in Mexico (Small, Short-nosed, and Hairless) and that the Indians ate these dogs as the Spanish do rabbits. The dogs intended for eating were castrated when very young so that they would grow fat.

While Hernandez was the first to write about them, Hernando de Soto and his men were the first to see the Small Indian Dog in great numbers. Entering Florida at Tampa Bay in 1539, de Soto headed an expedition that would cover most of the area of the southern United States. He crossed from what is now Florida to Mississippi and explored the area that became Arkansas and Oklahoma. He ended his expedition at the mouth of the Mississippi River. During this lengthy tour of exploration and conquest, the major source of meat was swine brought along by the party, horses as they fell or were maimed in battle, and Small Indian Dogs. Great numbers were needed to feed some five hundred men in the expedition, at least during the early phase. Later, when there were fewer men and the swine and horses were decimated, dogs became the major source of protein.

Typical events are reported by "Fidalgo of Elvas," a member of the Portuguese contingent of the expedition. Frequently, there would be a "scramble which would result when the army arrived in a town where there were only twenty or thirty dogs. And woe be unto the unsuccessful hunter who did not share his catch with his Captain." Garcilaso de la Vega, an Inca who recorded the exploits of de Soto, wrote that "for the general lack of meat in all that land, the Castilians ate as many dogs as they could lay hold of." How tasty the roast dog must have been to hungry troops. A scene of Spaniards engaged in butchering and cooking dog is shown on page 137. Painted by Miguel Gonzalez in the late 1600s as part of a commemorative plaque of the Hernando Cortes conquest of Mexico of 1519, it gives a vivid view of what must surely have been an excellent way to end a day's march.

The Spanish explorers and conquerors not only vanquished the tribes of the Southeast and Mesoamerican Indian Cultures but also brought havoc to the dog population. A small dog can feed but a few hungry men and there were hundreds to be fed every day. If one assumes that the Small Indian Dog was food for half of de Soto's six hundred men every other day during their three-year expedition, it is reasonable to believe that over one hundred thousand dogs were slaughtered. No wonder there was constant search as they moved across the Indian lands, and pleasure when a local chief provided dogs for food as did one who, as de la Vega wrote, "gave them three hundred of these animals." Such wholesale killing may account for the fact that when later explorers visited these same regions, there were hardly any Small Indian Dogs to be seen. Only from Florida and the northern states are there reports in the late eighteenth and early nineteenth centuries of this small breed. B. S. Barton describes dogs of the Florida Indians in 1805 as follows: "the latter had in addition to the larger dogs, a smaller breed, about the size of a fox." No doubt this was the Small Indian Dog and the first one mentioned was the Common Indian Dog described previously.

135

William Berczy's painting of the northern Indian Chief Joseph Brant with his Small Indian Dog, completed in 1797, is reproduced on the cover of this book. The Small Indian Dog is known to have been owned by the Northeast Woodland Tribes. The recorded description and the skeletal remains found at many an Indian refuse deposit in the northeast confirm the statement that the dog with Brant in the Berczy painting is a Small Indian Dog. The animal is fox-like, light limbed, with a narrow delicate head, has a fine muzzle, erect ears and a well-developed tail which is close-haired. Its colors are brown with white throat. These characteristics match those of the Small Indian Dog. Another painting of dogs and Indians is shown on page 124. Completed about 1820, this color lithograph by W. Day (after H. Jones) shows fox-like Ojibwa Indian Dogs dragging a toboggan near Lake Winnipeg. Whether they are Small Indian Dogs cannot be judged clearly, but a close look shows a number of typical features noted in descriptions of the Small Indian Dog.

Klamath-Indian Dog

Distribution: Among the Indians of the Klamath Lake region, south from Crater Lake to the California border. Also, occasionally among the Nomadic Indians of the Northern Plains.

Use: Household pets, for hunting and/or as sled dogs.

Appearance: Medium-sized, about 50 cm at the withers; erect ears; sharp muzzle; rough coat often with dark streaked gray coloring; tail short, about 15 cm, with bushy fur covering.

The isolated location that is the historic homeland of the Klamath Indians caused the tribe and their dogs to escape notice by the white frontier people for many years. The tribe has always occupied the valley region east of Mount McLoughlin and south of Mount Scott. Even today the tribe has its home on the Klamath Indian Reservation that is located south and east of Scott Mountain. Because of this geographic position, the early explorers and travelers missed the tribal area as they moved down the Columbia River far to the north, or down the Feather River in California to the south.

The first visitors to record the habits of the Klamath Indians and describe their special breed of dog were members of the exploratory and survey party of the United States Government engaged in locating possible railway routes from the Mississippi River to the Pacific Ocean.

136

Spaniards eating dog flesh during Cortes' march from Vera Cruz to Mexico City (Tenochtilan) in 1519. (A portion of a six-painting plaque attributed to Miquel Gonzalez. Late 1600s.)

The report, published in 1860, was written by George Suckley and George Gibbs. In their report they noted the existence of a unique breed and described it as follows: "On the Klamath is a dog of good size, with a short tail. This is not more than six or seven inches long, and is bushy, or rather broad, it being as wide as a man's hand. I was assured they were not cut, and I never noticed longer tails on the pups. They have the usual erect ears and short muzzle of Indian dogs, but are (what is unusual with Indian dogs) often brindled gray."

Allen believed that the breed was a variation of the Plains Indian Dog and that the shortened tail originated as a local variation and was preserved by selective breeding. There is some evidence that this may have happened, but the change could have been assisted by importation of short-tailed dogs from other tribes. Since it is reported that the Klamath-Indian Dog had, except for the tail, the general appearance of the Plains-Indian Dog, it is reasonable to look at the information about this latter breed for some clue as to the origin of this feature.

A Hidatsa Indian, Buffalo-Bird-Woman, who was born in 1840, some twenty years before the Klamath-Indian Dog was identified by Suckley and Gibbs, recalled the following as occurring during her youth.

There were a good many bobtailed dogs in the village, at least enough of them to make them common, although they were not as numerous as the others. There were perhaps about ten bobtailed dogs in the village. The bobtailed dog was born so and not made so artificially. A bobtailed dog or a dog with a tail like a wolf was equally good as a worker—it made no difference. My aunt had a bobtailed bitch which gave birth to a litter of puppies. I looked over the litter and found one that I liked very much and my aunt gave it to me. It was the first born of the whole litter, quite a large puppy, and was the only bobtailed puppy in the litter. I do not remember how many there were in the whole litter. The first-born puppies of a litter were always stronger and better dogs.

By repetitive selection of bobtailed dogs, a consistent type could be developed. Through trade, bobtailed dogs could have been acquired by Dakota, Crow, and Shoshoni tribal members during their many encounters as bordering neighbors. Since the short tail was a characteristic of all Klamath-Indian Dogs and, as reported by Buffalo-Bird-Woman, only appeared occasionally among the Hidatsa Indian Dogs, it is fair to assign the selective breeding and, therefore, origin of this type of dog to this western Indian tribe of Oregon.

138

Clallam-Indian Dog

Distribution: In the Puget Sound region from Tacoma to the Admiralty Inlet and west to Port Orchard. Along the coasts of Vancouver Island, on the east near Nanaimo, and on the west around Nootka Sound.

Use: Dense coat of fleece-like fur used as a source of material for woven products and blankets.

Appearance: Medium-sized; erect ears; woolly thick coat over entire head and body; bushy tail; coat white, occasionally light brown, perhaps black. Overall appearance like that of an unclipped Standard Poodle.

The Clallam-Indian Dog is probably the best authenticated and most interesting of the dogs of the American Indians. No doubt, this is because of the unique characteristics of the coat of the animal. The first to see the dog were the early explorers of the Vancouver area. Since they came by sea, they were able to move easily among the many islands and observe the lifestyle and the dogs of the local Indian tribes. Without the mobility that was offered by the many channels and bays, it is entirely possible that these dogs might have escaped close observation.

Selective breeding resulted in this unique animal and was surely influenced by the ecological conditions of the region. A damp, cool climate prevented the growing of crops suitable for the production of raw material for clothing. Additionally, big game was scarce and hunting of mountain goat was at best a difficult endeavor because of the remoteness from the tribes of the Puget Sound region. The alternative was to use a breed of dog with a wool-like coat suitable for twisting into thread. The result was the Clallam-Indian Dog shown on page 141. These paintings, made by Paul Kane in the mid-1800s while visiting the Salish and Strait of Juan de Fuca tribes, give an excellent view of this woolly-coated Poodle-like dog.

The Puget Sound women wove on vertical looms of local design. Additionally, they employed a unique hand-held stick-spinner to draw the dog wool into thick ropes. The dog wool thread was used in the making of blankets, hats, and leggings. The lower illustration on page 141 shows the weaving of blankets. The vertical warp was made of twisted mountain-goat hair and milkweed fiber, while the thick weft was twisted dog wool. The first to record the herding of the Clallam-Indian Dogs and the making of woven products was George Vancouver, who surveyed the region for Great Britain in the early 1790s. While at the Port Orchard harbor in May 1792, Vancouver wrote:

139

The dogs belonging to this tribe of Indians were numerous, and much resembled those of Pomerania, though in general somewhat larger. They were all shorn as close to the skin as sheep are in England; and so compact were their fleeces, that large portions could be lifted up by a corner without causing any separation. They were composed of a mixture of a coarse kind of wool, with very fine long hair, capable of being spun into yarn.

While Vancouver may have been puzzled by the extensive use of dog wool, others have noted without hesitation that herds of medium sized white woolly dogs were owned by women who kept them separated from other dogs. Even Vancouver relates in his report seeing "families, and others walking along the shore (on Puget Island), attended by about forty dogs in a drove shorn close to the skin like sheep." This was in June when spring shearing would have been completed.

Some forty years later, C. Hamilton Smith, a British naturalist, reported that the Clallam-Indian Dog was a large dog "with pointed upright ears, docile, but chiefly valuable on account of the immense load of fur it bears on the back, of white, and brown, and black colours, but having the woolly proportion so great and fine, that it may well be called a fleece."

Some twenty years later, George Suckley stated positively that "all the Clallam dogs that I saw were pure white; but they have the sharp nose, pointed ear, and heavy-dog, thievish appearance of other Indian dogs."

These comments about the features raise the question of the origin of the breed. Since the dogs remained on islands, one can assume that the breed was not inclined to enter water. It is known that Siberian and Eskimo Dogs have an abhorrence for entering water. No doubt this trait was reinforced in the Clallam-Indian Dog from the hazards of immersion in the extremely cold waters of the region. The locale of the Clallam-Indian Dog, with a long, yet entirely possible, access by way of the coastal waterways to Alaska, could have permitted movement of the original breed stock from the Arctic.

No doubt the Salish Indians took advantage of the natural instincts of the dog to maintain the breed separately to develop its special features, and to prevent crossing with other breeds of Indian dogs. As late as 1866, the breed was still prized by the coastal tribes near Vancouver.

Unfortunately, by the early 1900s the breed was extinct. When the Hudson Bay Company began selling blankets to the Indians, the need for dog wool ended. The native weaving industry ceased, along with the selective breeding and herding of the Clallam-Indian Dog.

Above: In a portion of a painting by Paul Kane, breed characteristics are shown clearly in this young Clallam-Indian Dog. (Royal Ontario Museum.)

Below: Portion of an 1852 painting by Paul Kane of Northwest Coast Clallam Indians and their white Poodle-like dog. (Royal Ontario Museum.)

Mexican Hairless Dog, called Lupus Mexicanus, as shown in the book written by Francisco Hernandez and published in 1651 by Recchi and Lynceus.

142

Southwest Dogs

Short-nosed Indian Dog

Distribution: Widespread among the Indians of southern North America from Florida and Virginia across to California. Also in northwestern South America from Venezuela across to Peru. Disappeared before the arrival of European explorers in the early sixteenth century.

Use: No confirmed use. Small size would indicate major role was as a household pet.

Appearance: A compactly built dog, the size of a small Terrier; erect ears; high forehead with rounded skull; short heavy muzzle; short body and limbs; short rough coat of black and white or yellowish with dark blotched fur.

While only skeletal remains and descriptive writings are available to define most dogs of the American aborigines, we have an entirely different situation for the Short-nosed Indian Dog! There have been but a few occasions in the history of archeology when the investigators in the field have chanced upon very special finds of entire, desiccated specimens. Most often these have been mummified humans.

Interestingly, though, at two places in North America and one in South America, field investigations have uncovered the remains of mummified dogs. Surprisingly, both locations contain the well preserved remains, including full coat, of the Short-nosed Indian Dog. In a burial performed sometime after the period of the Cliff Dwellers, an adult black and white Short-nosed Indian Dog was interred near Kayenta, Arizona. The discovery was made by S. J. Guernsey in White Cave near Marsh Pass and reported in 1921. About 1880, archeological investigators from Germany discovered remains of the same breed in the prehistoric cemetery of Ancon in Peru. The White Cave Dog is shown on page 65 along with a Long-haired Pueblo Dog found in the same burial. Allen, who studied the remains, described the Short-nosed Indian Dog:

143

The other dog is a much smaller, black-and-white individual, about the size of a terrier, with short, but not close, shaggy coat, erect ears, and long full-haired tail. Its muzzle is rather short and stubby in contrast to the fine slender muzzle of other Indian dogs of about the same size. In common with many skulls of American Indian dogs, the first premolar is lacking in the adult dentition of the lower jaw. This specimen is of especial interest as establishing beyond doubt the identity of certain dog bones from Ely Cave, Virginia . . . for they agree perfectly with corresponding parts of the Arizona dog. An identical breed is represented among the mummified remains of dogs from the necropolis of Ancon, Peru . . . . Evidently it had a wide distribution in our south and southwest, and was known also to the Peruvians. I have called this the Short-nosed Indian Dog.

The White Cave animal was owned by the Pueblo Basketmaker II Indians about 500 B.P. It and the larger white-coated dog, shown on page 65, were found in stone-lined burial pits along with mummies of human adults and an infant. All were covered by flat carrying baskets.

The mummified Short-nosed Indian Dog from Peru was also exhumed with human mummies. These two similar burials, although separated so far in distance, occurred at about the same time. Fate and a preserving dry climate made it possible for their lifelike remains to be viewed and studied by us hundreds of years later!

As Allen mentions, the White Cave mummified specimen is positively related to a dog whose bones were found in Ely Cave, Virginia. The bones were obtained during excavation of the top layer of earth in the Ely Cave by Dr. J. A. Allen in 1885. The bones were quite fresh in appearance and only slightly discolored, indicating a rather recent burial, in archeological terms. The remains of Indian occupation were numerous. The dog bones were small size. Of particular interest was the humerus, which lacked the circular hole at the middle of the bone near the elbow joint. This perforation is a usual feature of the humerus of all modern dogs, and prehistoric dogs, wolves, and coyotes.

Allen cut into the White Cave specimen through the dried tissue at the elbow and exposed the humerus in the area where the large hole usually is found. He found but a tiny hole in the right humerus and but two small pores side-by-side in the left humerus. Since the dog was a young animal, Allen concluded that the perforation would have closed in a few years and the area would have looked like that of the bones found at Ely Cave. He concluded, "so complete is the correspondence of the bones (of the Ely Cave Dog) . . . with those of the prehistoric dog of Arizona that they may

144

be unhesitatingly pronounced those of a similar if not identical breed of Indian Dog." Equally significant, the dog bones from Ancon, Peru, also exhibit the same thick humerus and lack of any trace of the usual hole. Clearly, this is a diagnostic feature that confirms the presence of this small dog at widely separated locations.

San Nicolas Island, California, is a fourth location and Crystal River, Florida, a fifth place where skeletal remains of the Short-nosed Indian Dog were found. Measurements of the skull and other bones of dogs from these sites and the locations in Peru, Arizona, and Virginia were made by Allen and show surprising uniformity. Allen reports:

Length, occiput to medium incisor ....138 mm
Canine incisor to second molar.........................60 mm
Width of palate outside first molar ....56 mm
Zygomatic width......................................86 mm
Width of occipital condyles............................30 mm
Ulna ....120 mm
Humerus ....97 mm
Tibia...116 mm
Femur ....106 mm

They are characterized by their broad brain-cases, spreading zygomata, wide palates, shortened rostra, and small teeth. In profile the dorsal outline of the brain-case is gently rounded, not flat. The shortness of the rostrum does not amount to real deformity, however, for the lower jaw closes normally into its place and the premolars are not markedly crowded .... The dogs are small, about the size of a Fox-terrier but more compactly and heavily built, with a shorter head, erect ears, and longer tail. (The White Cave Dog fur) still shows a black and white pattern, with a narrow median white line from nose to forehead, with a white chin, throat, and belly, a white collar, white feet, and tail tip. Much of the body is black.

These comments by Allen and the great similarity in the skeletal formation and size, particularly the closed form of the humerus, are ample evidence to confirm conclusively the presence of this unique breed of Indian dog in the Americas prior to the arrival of the European explorers.

Long-haired Pueblo Dog
Distribution: Common to the Pueblo tribes of Arizona and New Mexico, and the Marsh Pass region near Kayenta, Arizona.

145

Use: Dense coat of long woolly hair used as a source material for woven products. As a household pet for young children and women.

Appearance: Medium-sized with slender muzzle, erect ears, and bushy tail. Coat wool-like, long and dense, pale yellow with touch of brown on ears and top of head, whitish under belly, chest, and legs. Longish matted hair on feet. Judged to be a long-haired version of the Plains-Indian Dog.

Investigators S. J. Guernsey and A. V. Kidder discovered the dried remains of the Long-haired Pueblo Dog and the Short-nosed Indian Dog, which are shown on page 65. These rare finds were associated with human burial in White Cave near Kayenta, Arizona. The Indian remains were dated to shortly after the time of the Cliff Dwellers, about five hundred years ago.

The origin of indigenous southwestern Indian dogs was studied by Harold S. Colton in the mid-1960s. He compared skeletal material of dogs in the collections of the Museums of Arizona with twenty-seven skeletons of southwestern dogs that had been studied previously by William G. Haag. Of special importance were the nasal to occiptal measurement of the skulls, and the humerus and femur lengths. These measurements permitted the clear identification of small and large dogs in this area of the Southwest.

Small dogs had median skull lengths of 140 mm, while the large dog skull median was 180 mm with a range from 165 to 196 mm. Colton judged the smaller dogs to be Short-nosed Indian Dogs. He noted that the large dogs had significantly larger muzzles than the small dogs. Noting the age of the skeletal remains led to the conclusion that the large dogs arrived from the Great Plains some time after A.D. 800 and existed up to about A.D. 1600. In many respects the skeletal remains of the large dogs were similar to those of the Plains-Indian Dog. Colton and Allen judged it to be the original stock that was selectively bred to have long hair. The specimen found in White Cave is about the size of a Plains-Indian Dog but differs markedly in color and length of coat. These long coated dogs were bred by the Pueblo Indians. Their number increased as the fortunes of their Indian owners improved, reaching their greatest number around A.D. 1200 to A.D. 1300. This "classic" period of the Pueblos produced the "cliff dwellings" and the terraced apartment house complexes. Crops included squash, beans, varicolored corn, tobacco, and cotton. Handsome pottery, and blankets woven on tall, upright looms, were in common use. The need was great for long woolly dog hair to be combined with the short cotton fibers for weaving. The considerable number of large dog skeletons of this era is evidence of this role for the Long-haired Pueblo Dog.

This high period for this breed of dog gradually ended as a creeping drought cycle began and reached into the 1500s. The cliff villages were gradually abandoned and, with shortages of food and water, dissension and war caused a diminished life style. By the time of Coronado's advance from Mexico across the Southwest in 1540, the Pueblo Indians were poverty ridden and the Long-haired Pueblo Dog was a rare breed. The use of the coat as a wool stock eventually would serve only special needs. Shortly, even this role would end, since, with the arrival in 1599 of Don Juan de Onate, came sheep and goats.

Coronado's view of the Long-haired Indian Dog is confirmed in correspondence by his companion, Mendoza, in a letter dated April 17, 1540, addressed to the King of Spain. Describing the Pueblo Indians that were encountered at the Pueblo of Cibola, then a famous Indian site near the present town of Zuni, New Mexico, Mendoza writes, "In their houses they keep some hairy animals, like the large Spanish hounds, which they shear, and they make long colored wigs from the hair, like this one which I send to Your Lordship, which they wear, and they also put this same stuff into the cloth they make."

Mendoza also notes that the men wore "a cloak" and the women "shirts or chemises which reach down to their feet," and that these garments were made of the mixture of cotton and dog hair. Unfortunately, there is no longer a record of the "long colored wigs" such as the one Mendoza send to his "Lordship."

Of the Long-haired Indian Dog "hair," we have excellent evidence from the White Cave mummified specimen that is dated at less than one hundred years before Coronado's arrival in the area. The thick hair over this entire animal is described by Allen: "It is covered with a dense coat of long woolly hair, of a pale yellowish color, clouded on the back and head with brownish. On the sides of the body, the length of the hair is about 100 mm; on the toes 30 mm."

The keeping of long-haired dogs for shearing was not confined to the Pueblo Indians. It will be shown that Indians of the Puget Sound area and of the southern coast of Chile also engaged in such husbandry to obtain weaving material.

The arid climate of the Southwest caused the White Cave specimen to be preserved excellently. The condition of the mummy was studied very carefully by Allen because of the rarity of the find. He was able to measure the specimen, but was somewhat limited due to the rigid and desiccated condition. Nevertheless, he reported the following external

147

measurements for this breed which, interestingly, can be compared with long-haired dogs of today. In many ways, the Long-haired Indian Dog is like the Collie breed, as will be noted from the following data:

Length from nose to root of tail, following backbone .....700 mm
Length of tail (broken at tip) slightly over ....200 mm
Hind foot ....141 mm
Femur (approximately) ....145 mm
Tibia (approximately)...............................143 mm
Upper jaw, front of canine to back of pm4............. 55.5 mm
Upper carnassial ....18 mm
Length of skull from occiput to tip of nose (approximate). 195 mm
Width outside upper canines ....31 mm
Width outside upper carnassials ....54 mm
Zygomatic width (about) ....95 mm
Lower jaw, front of canine to back of mi .... 68.5 mm
Lower jaw, front of canine to back of p4 ....49 mm
Lower jaw, pm1 to pm4 ....35 mm
Length of lower carnassial ....21 mm

Mexican Hairless Dog

Distribution: From Northern Mexico to Peru in the lower elevations, although sparse in the central region. Also possibly on some of the islands of the Greater Antilles (i.e. Jamaica) and among the Indians of Paraguay.

Use: As a household pet. As food. As a source of heat to reduce the pains from muscular ache and rheumatism.

Appearance: Medium-sized, rather heavily built and with large body; erect ears, rather large for size of head; thick tail usually carried drooping between legs; rough skinned without hair except at tip of tail and sometimes on crown of head; skin usually a slate gray or reddish gray color, paler on upper legs with possible white blotches at lower portions.

Some confusion exists about the origin of the Mexican Hairless Dog. Naturalists of the early 1800s considered the animal to be the same as the Turkish and Egyptian Hairless Dog. They implied that it had been brought to Middle America by early explorers and traders. Today we have a different view based principally on the work of Allen. His studies of aboriginal dogs led him to judge the Mexican Hairless as an indigenous

148

breed. He concluded that it was "most likely a variant of the larger type of Indian Dog, in which the hairlessness is due to a retention of the embryonic condition of the skin, precluding hair development just as the short-nosed breeds of dogs are the result of the failure of the facial bones to attain full growth."

Based on his extensive knowledge of the different types of dogs around the world, he judged the Middle European Hairless to be "a hairless variety of another breed" and not related in any way to the Mexican Hairless Dog.

Allen, of course, had firsthand knowledge of residual specimens that still possess, even today, basic characteristics of the breed. This was in addition to descriptions prepared by early explorers. Francisco Hernandez, who lived in Mexico in the 1500s, was the first to describe the dogs of the country. He noted that there were three types that were in his time kept by the Indians. Of the three, only the Mexican Hairless was known to him positively since he states that he had seen it personally. He called it the "Xoloytzcuintli" and described it as being fairly large, about three feet long of body, but with the odd feature of having no hair, although covered with soft slate colored skin that was at times spotted.

This excellent description is even faithful to the present-day members of this ancient breed. Recchi and Lynceus, who published the work of Hernandez in 1651, added information based on their own firsthand knowledge and included an etching of the dog. The illustration on page 142 shows the dog that they described as fierce and wolf-like, with a few bristles on the muzzle, but no other hair.

The dog in this old picture from Recchi and Lynceus can be compared with the dog shown in the lower illustration, a Mexican Hairless Dog that was photographed by Arthur Stockdale in 1917. It is truly amazing that a breed given so little systematic attention for over two hundred years should retain its uniqueness. As with the Eskimo Dog, it must have possessed some particularly valuable trait which led to its being bred continuously without change up to the present time. Since there are no records of a special role to ensure survival in a harsh climate, one can only conjecture to explain the durability of the breed. Maybe roast Hairless Dog was especially good, or perhaps the 105-degree Fahrenheit warmth radiating from the hairless hide was especially soothing to aches and pains.

The lack of hair would be attractive to the Indians but a problem for the dog. Even today the Mexican Hairless Dog is extremely sensitive to changes in temperature. For this reason, it usually is found in the lower altitudes. Even then, care must be taken. Almost one hundred years ago

149

E. Seler observed that "the Mexican wrapped these dogs in cloth at night as a protection against cold." While in Peru in 1844, J. J. von Tschudi observed, "this dog is mainly on the coast, since its lack of a hairy coat made it unable to withstand the cold of the higher altitudes of the interior except in the warm valleys and then only if carefully protected."

Without a hair covering, the dog also was an easy prey for all sorts of flying insects, especially flies. This was observed by Stockdale during his photography (the example of which is seen on page 140). Yet the same hairlessness would be an advantage in preventing the infestation with crawling insects. Throughout the Americas, early observers of Indian Dogs frequently commented on the fact that the dogs were flea- and tick-ridden. While the Mexican Hairless Dog may have needed a blanket to keep warm, and a twitching, now and then, to put the flies to flight, it was surely free of the need to scratch and chew to dislodge biting and sucking insects. The hairlessness may, in fact, have been essential for survival in the insect infested region of Central America, home ground of the Mexican Hairless Dog.

Alternatively, its survival may have been related to the burial practices of the native Indians. Earlier it was noted that clay dogs were used as grave furniture. These plump dog sculptures have features similar to those of the Mexican Hairless Dog. The sculpture shown on page 67, of a native woman suckling a young dog, is judged to be over thirty-five hundred years old. This sculpture predates the Colima civilization by eighteen hundred years. If we accept the similarity between these clay replicas, the historic descriptions, and the present-day examples of the breed, it can be said almost with certainty that the Mexican Hairless Dog is the oldest unchanged breed in America!

Mexican Hairless Dog, described first by Francisco Hernandez about 1550. He called it the "Xoloytzcuintli." (Photograph by Arthur Stockdale, 1917.)

Sketch of Inca Dog with Inca girl diligently spinning while both attend the herd of llamas. (By Guaman Poma de Ayala, seventeenth century.)

Inca Indian Dogs

Inca Dog

Distribution: Along the western coast of South America from northwest Argentina to northern Peru.

Use: As a guard dog; to track and capture game birds; to herd lamoids (members of the camel family).

Appearance: Medium-sized, square with strong body; legs rather short; heavy skull in proportion to size of body, with narrow muzzle; coat rough, long and thick with dark yellow color; inner sides of limbs of a lighter shade than on back; tail about two-thirds the length of the body, fully haired and curved forward.

The dogs of the Inca Indians, like those of the Pueblo Indians, are unique in that they are available for study as mummified specimens. In the late 1800s, archeologist Alfred Nehring excavated the ancient Peruvian cemetery of Ancon, Peru, and unearthed mummified remains of a number of dogs of two types. One was the Inca Dog, while the other was the Long-haired Inca Dog. Later, in 1915, G. F. Eaton discovered dog mummies with pre-Columbian period human burials at Machu Picchu, Peru. The Inca Dog is the largest of the Peruvian dogs—about the size of a small Collie, but more heavily proportioned.

The dogs of Ancon were described by Nehring in 1884 as having hair a pale yellowish in color with darker areas. The hair was dense and thickest on the neck and breast, forming a mane. The ears of most of the specimens were clipped. This is the only instance of American Indian dogs with this feature and may be related to certain religious rites of the Incas.

The Incas' regard for the dog is shown by the many figures of dogs carved on their amulets. Examples in the collection of the University Museum at Cuzco, Peru, show a short-haired, medium-sized, short-legged dog with sharp pointed face and tail curled up over the back. This dog was used by the Incas during seasonal drives to corral the various

153

members of the camel (lamoid) family that inhabit the South American Andes. The llama, alpaca, guanaco, and vicuna are of value for wool and food and were hunted and herded by the ancient Peruvian Indians. A reasonable image of the Inca Dog in association with a herd of llamas is shown on page 152. This sketch was made in the late 1600s by the Inca writer, Guraman Poma de Oyala. The dog in the figure, while small in size compared to the girl and the llamas, is a good representative of the breed.

The largest of the Inca Dogs found at Ancon had a skull about 172 mm long, humerus 147 mm, ulna 172 mm, and radius 140 mm. A full mummy had a head and body length of 660 mm, with a tail, including hair, of 240 mm. The average zygomatic width for six Inca Dog specimens is 100 mm, while the breadth across the occipital condylis is 34 mm. It is interesting to note that the largest skull of the six is almost exactly the same as a skull of a Common Indian Dog collected by Robert Kennicott in 1800 from Peel River, Alaska. The only difference is the narrower portion of the skull across the occipital condyles in the Inca Dog. This is judged by Allen to result from a lack of development of neck and shoulder muscles since these dogs were not used to haul travois or sleds. The general similarity of skull and skeletal proportions with those of the Common Indian Dog indicates a close genetic relationship to these larger dogs of North America.

It was still possible in the late 1800s to see Inca Dogs around every Indian hut in the highland of Peru, and accompanying every Indian shepherd. Travelers reported that Inca Dogs seemed to have a special dislike of white people. Most Europeans, as they approached on horseback, were charged by the dogs, which attempted to leap up and bite the travelers' legs. The dogs were fearless in their attack and would fight an enemy, whether man or beast, with courage and determination. Yet to their owners, they were noted as excellent pets that were easily trained to hunt and herd. Today, they are all gone except for the few strays that can be found running free on the back streets of Cuzco and as members of native family groups in the back area highlands of South America.

Long-haired Inca Dog

Distribution: Found originally along the western coastal area of Peru, south to the Taitao Peninsula, Chile.

Use: Principally as a source of hair used in the making of woven coverings for native wear in inclement weather.

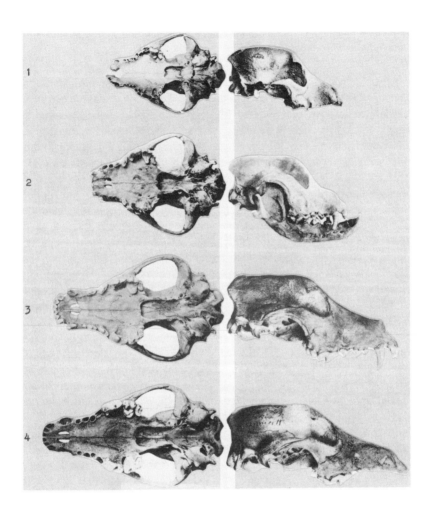

Skulls representative of range in size and conformation of dogs of the American Indians:

1. Short-nosed Indian Dog (138 mm)—Saint Nicholas Island, California.
2. Peruvian Pug-nosed Dog (147 mm)—Huacho, Peru.
3. Inca Dog (168 mm)—Huacho, Peru.
4. Common Indian Dog (190 mm)—Yukon, Canada.

Appearance: In size and shape similar to the ordinary Inca Dog, but with long hair, especially on feet and tail; pelage color dull yellow.

This Long-haired Inca Dog was first identified in the mid-1500s by the Spanish explorers Giocueta and Del Techo. The expedition that explored the coast of Peru and Chile sailed to the Taitao Peninsula at about forty-five degrees south latitude. To the north, they found the Chonos Indians who inhabited the coastal region. Wretchedly poor shell-fish gatherers with little material wealth, they raised a few potatoes and ate wild plants and small game. Since the Chilean waters had virtually no fish and there was little wild game, the life of the Chonos Indians was extremely harsh. Charles Darwin, who studied the life style of the natives of southern Chile, considered them to be the most miserable of humans. Fortunately, they had one saving possession: the Long-haired Dog. The Spanish explorers who were members of the Cortes Hojia expedition of 1553-54 reported the existence along the coast of a breed of long-haired shaggy dogs, from the hair of which the Chonos Indians wove mantles that they used to cover the upper portion of their bodies. This poncho-shaped short cloak was the main garment in winter.

The Long-haired Inca Dog was a vital partner in the survival patterns of the Chonos Indians. The dog was probably an offshoot from the larger Collie-like Inca Dog found among the ancient Peruvians to the north. In fact, the Long-haired Inca Dog must have been more common in earlier times since a well-preserved specimen was found by Alfred Nehring during his excavations at Ancon, Peru, in the early 1880s. The mummified dog was found with feet tied to head and wrapped in a cloth made of tree-wool. Allen judged the dog to be similar to the Long-haired Pueblo Dog found at Marsh Pass, Arizona, by Guernsey and Kidder. The hair of the Inca Dog was unusually long, especially on the feet and tail. The mummified animal's hair was dull yellow in color, while its skull and leg bone indicated a slender canine. In overall appearance, the Long-haired Inca Dog resembled the modern Collie.

It is interesting that the Long-haired Inca Dog is the third of the dogs of the American Indians that was bred as a source of raw material for the making of cloth. The Clallam-Indian Dogs and the Long-haired Pueblo Dogs also served this purpose. In all cases the lack of a desirable or conveniently available alternate for body coverings caused the Indians to look to the dog for help. Along the coastal regions of the forty-five to fifty degree latitudes of both North and South America, the lack of large game deprived the Indians of skins and furs for clothing.

156

Similarly, in the desert region of southwestern North America, the scarcity of large wild animals caused the Pueblo Indians to innovate in making clothing. The Clallam and other Pacific Coast Indians used cedar bark strips, bird feathers, and Rocky Mountain sheep wool to supplement the dog wool as material for weaving. The South American coastal Indians added wool from the lamoids (the llama, alpaca, guanaco, and vicuna) to the hair of the Long-haired Inca Dog in order to weave coverings. One can accept easily the reason the dog was bred to have a wool-like coat when it is recognized that the Indians would have a difficult time capturing the swift traveling birds, mountain goats, or lamoids. How much easier life must have been after the earliest dog breeding specialist created an abundance of friendly animals with fine long hair for weaving.

Approximate areas where various breeds of Indian Dogs were to be found in Central and South America.

Southern South American Dogs

Peruvian Pug-nosed Dog

Distribution: Found only in the Peruvian Highlands in ancient burial sites at Ancon, Huacho, and Pachacamac.

Use: Not definitely known; small size of dog based on the size of the head indicates a family pet or house dog to scare off rodents and trespassers.

Appearance: Head similar in shape and size to that of the Bulldog, body similar to the Short-nosed Indian Dog; color of coat yellowish or whitish, marked with dark brown patches.

The Peruvian Pug-nosed Dog was first discovered by archeologists working at burial sites at Ancon, Peru. Alfred Nehring published accounts of the work in 1885. Later, discoveries were made at other sites in the Peruvian Highlands by members of the Yale-National Geographic Society Expedition. It came as a distinct surprise to the investigators to find skulls of pug-nosed dogs that were similar to dogs of the European Middle Ages yet had derived independently. The Peruvian Pug-nosed Dog predated by hundreds of years any known intercourse with the Old World.

The skull of one of the Peruvian dogs found at Huacho is shown on page 155, along with the skulls of the Short-nosed Indian, Inca, and Common Indian Dogs. The sizes of the four skulls, ranging in occipitonostral length from 137 to 190 mm and the variations in overall shape, demonstrate clearly the uniqueness of the Peruvian Pug-nosed Dog. Its short facial bones, undershot lower jaw, broad zygomata, and large nasal region are distinct characteristics. Shortening of the face results in an elevated forehead and a deep "stop."

The origin of this dog is a mystery, although Allen concluded after studying the remains that it was probably derived from the Short-nosed Dog of North America. It is conceivable that the Peruvian Dog was the result of crossbreeding between a few North American dogs obtained in trade and some small version of the local Inca Dog. Once obtained, either

159

by purposeful or chance breeding, the characteristic dog was preserved by continued selective matings to result in a new breed known today as the Peruvian Pug-nosed Dog.

Patagonian Dog

Distribution: From the Strait of Magellan in South Chile, through the Santa Cruz Province and northward across Patagonia to the Rio Colorado Province of Argentina.

Use: As an aid to hunters in pursuit of the guanaco, the South American ostrich and other small animals; as a guard dog and as a family pet to entertain the children.

Appearance: A medium-sized dog, about the size of an English Foxhound; coat usually short and wiry, although sometimes longish; color of coat uniformly dark with occasional spots; wolfish in appearance yet resembling the Belgian Shepherd Dog; tall, slender, with attentive stare and bushy tail.

While many explorers sailed around Cape Horn at the southern tip of South America or used the Strait of Magellan for a shorter passage, their stops along the coast to the north on the Atlantic side were few indeed. Inhospitable climate and geography permitted only a sparse Indian population and provided no reason for stopping. Even today only dire circumstances prompt a ship to seek port along this barren five hundred mile coastline. Fortunately for the history of the dog, a serious problem arose during the southern passage of the famous "Beagle," the main sailing ship of the Darwin around-the-world expedition. The stop at the mouth of the Santa Cruz River to repair the hull permitted Darwin to make a side journey up the river and into the Patagonian interior.

It was during this stop that Midshipman Philip King made the sketch of Tehuelche Indians and their dogs shown on page 161. Drawn in 1834, it is the only representation that exists of the Patagonian Dog. Fortunately, it shows details that are in full accord with the description prepared later by Captain Robert Fitzroy, master of the "Beagle."

Writing to British naturalist Hamilton Smith in 1840, Captain Fitzroy described the Patagonian Dog as an animal about the size of a large, strong Foxhound. He noted that its coat was usually short and wiry. The wolfish appearance, resulting no doubt from the upstanding pointed ears and dark tan or black coat, was also described. These features are all quite apparent in the illustration, which shows four very similarly formed and

Tehuelche Indians and Patagonian Dogs meet members of the Darwin Expedition during their visit to the Santa Cruz Province, Argentina, in 1834. This sketch by Midshipman Philip King first appeared in the Voyage Narrative by Captain Robert FitzRoy.

coated canines. It is obvious that they were bred to a type with long limbs and deep large chests.

These characteristics of the dogs in the sketch drawn by King imply vigor and alertness, qualities that would be necessary in the chase. Throughout the whole region of Patagonia, the tribal groups depended on hunting and gathering for their survival. The diet of roots and herbs was supplemented with the flesh of the guanaco, rhea, and small rodents. The camel-like guanaco and the ostrich-like rhea are exceedingly fast. Dogs, swift and large, would be needed by the Tehuelche Indians to make the kill, and only a dog with such characteristics would be useful and worth keeping in a region that could barely support the Indian owners.

Conditions in Patagonia were so harsh that the native population was among the sparsest in South America and did not survive past the late 1800s. The dogs too have vanished and no bones are available for study. Their origin is obscure but because of their size, it is reasonable to assume that they were derived from the same basic stock as the Inca Dog. One small bit of evidence exists that might be linked with the Patagonian Dogs seen by Darwin. In 1913, archeologist Herman von Ihering found the skull of a prehistoric dog in the northwestern portion of Argentina, some six hundred miles from Santa Cruz and at the furthest end of the Patagonian ecologic system. When compared to the Inca Dog, it was found to be decidedly larger. Its occipitorostral length was 190 mm, the same as the Larger or Common Indian Dog shown on page 163 and described earlier, evidence that this bit of skeletal remains could have been from a forerunner of the Patagonian Dogs seen by Darwin and his shipmates in 1834.

Fuegian Dog

Distribution: Along the western shores of Tierra del Fuego and lesser Islands of the Fuegian Archipelago, from Cape Horn to Beagle Channel, and northwestward at least to the western reaches of the Magellan Strait.

Use: Principally, as an aid for hunting sea otters and to dive and chase fish into nets; also as a watchdog, having a loud, sharp bark; as a faithful companion to its master and comforter of women and children; as a source of warmth.

Appearance: Small but square, standing about 40 cm at the withers; slender limbs; short, powerful neck with shoulders slightly higher than rump; large, pointed, erect ears on a broad head; ears mobile and directed

162

A man of the Tekeenica tribe and his Tierro Del Fuego Dog. (Sketched by Conrad Martens, 1832.)

163

forward; very sharp, slender muzzle; feet webbed between the toes; tail bushy and carried high; coat short; color variable, often uniformly grayish-tan or black or tan on a white background; white spot over each eyebrow with a few projecting tawny colored hairs.

Of all the Indians of both North and South America, those that lived along the western shores of the southernmost islands of Chile were the most dependent upon their dogs for survival. While we have seen that many tribes had dogs and used them for various purposes such as for hunting, protection, and even food, none were so important to their masters as the Fuegian Dog. It also can be said that none were trained as carefully and in such unique ways.

The special relationships that existed between the Fuegian Dog and the Ona, Yahgan, and Alacaluf Indians were, no doubt, the result of living in what is judged by many to be the most unpleasant climate on earth. The Fuegian Archipelago has summer temperatures in the fifty-degree Fahrenheit range with monotonous cloud cover. Rain squalls are the norm with only now and then a bright day. In winter, temperatures are at or below freezing with sleet and wet snow the norm. It is difficult to imagine why any native would want to live under such harsh conditions, yet existing along the coastal ways for centuries was a population of a few thousand hardy souls and their dogs.

Darwin called them "the most miserable humans he had ever seen." Even more surprising, they were hardly clothed and seemed perpetually to be out in the weather or in the sea. Even though the water ranged from forty to fifty degrees Fahrenheit, the Indians had a tolerance for cold that was a marvel to all who observed their life style. It was noted by Bryon, of the Darwin expedition, that he "frequently observed in the children of these savages, who, even at the age of three years, might be seen crawling upon their hands and knees among the rocks and breakers, from which they would tumble themselves into the sea, without regard to the cold, which is often intense, and showing no fear of the noise and roaring of the surf."

Surely this was exceptional training and hardened the body. It would permit in later life the diving into twenty to thirty feet of water that was common for the women in taking from the sea bottom mollusks and sea urchins for food. An equally demanding task for the men was wading for an hour or so in waist-deep water to net fish and spear seals. It was in this latter endeavor that the Fuegian Dogs performed uniquely. Over the years they had been developed, through selective breeding by the natives, to be willing and able to herd fish! As Bryon wrote in 1830,

"These dogs are a cur-like looking animal, but very sagacious, and easily trained to this business. Though, in appearance, an uncomfortable sort of sport, yet they engage in it readily, seem to enjoy it much, and express their eagerness by barking every time they raise their heads above the water to breathe. The net is held by two Indians, who get into the water; then the dogs, taking a large compass, dive after the fish, and drive them into the net."

On another occasion, Bryon stated that the natives "had taught their dogs to drive the fish into a corner of some pond, or lake, from whence they were easily taken out by the skill and address of these savages."

These accounts show how invaluable their service was to their masters in the search for food, not only as fish herders but also as underwater pursuers of sea otters. Captain Fitzroy of the Darwin Expedition described the natives' ability in killing otters and seals by spearing them after they had been driven close to their boats by the dogs.

The Fuegians so prized their dogs that the oldest women of the tribe were sacrificed to satisfy the dogs' hunger rather than kill a single dog. It was said that "Dogs catch otter, old women are good for nothing." The love for the dog and male dominance began at very early ages, as can be judged from this tale by Captain P. Parker King:

I took a fancy to a dog lying near one of the women, and offered a price for it; one of my seamen, supposing the bargain concluded, laid hands on the dog, at which the woman set up a dismal yell; so bidding him desist, I increased my offers. She declined to part with it, but would give two others. At last, my offers became so considerable, that she called a little boy out of the thick jungle (into which he had fled at our approach), who was the owner of the dog. The goods were shown to him, and all his party urged him to sell it, but the little urchin would not consent. He offered to let me have his necklace, and what he received in exchange was put away in his own little basket.

But what kind of a dog was this extra special canine? Fortunately we have two sketches, made about fifty years apart, that show details of the Fuegian Dog. While with Darwin in 1832, Conrad Martens made the sketch shown on page 163 of a native of the Tekeenica tribe and his dog. Easily seen are the characteristic sharp pointed, erect, and high-set ears that are directed forward in a bat-like manner. We can see why the overall appearance and pointed muzzle caused Fitzroy, in a letter to Hamilton Smith in 1840, to describe the dog as resembling "a mixture of fox, shepherd's dog and terrier." In 1883, two Fuegian Dogs from the

Yahgan tribe were brought back to France by Dr. Huades of the Mission Scientifique au Cap Horn. One of these animals is shown in the sketch on page 167. The dog is described by the French investigator d'Herculais as having a "fox-like head with pointed muzzle, broad forehead, its erect and high-set ears, usually directed forward, very mobile; eyes slightly oblique. The body is large, limbs slender, the neck short and powerful, the shoulders slightly higher than the rump; tail bushy and carried high. Pelage with a short under fur, pied black and white, passing to slaty at the throat, clouded with tan; over each eyebrow a white spot with a few fulvous hairs."

Measurements of these Fuegian Dogs were:

Scapuloischial length	52 mm
Height at shoulder	45 mm
Height at rump	43 mm
Height at axila	25 mm
Thoracic perimeter	58 mm
Distance between ears	9 mm
Distance between eyes	8.5 mm
Breadth of forehead	11 mm
Length of head	22 mm
Length of muzzle	9 mm
Condylo-incisive length	141 mm
Length of palate	71.3 mm
Canine to back of m2	64 mm
Length of premolar	15.2 mm
Width of palate outside m1	52.6 mm
Zygomatic width	81 mm
Length of humerus	105 mm
Length of ulna	125 mm
Length of femur	132 mm
Length of tibia	139 mm

From nose to end of tail, they measured about 76 cm, while the tail was about 75 cm. The pups grew up in France and were reported to be tame and affectionate. They were active animals, strong in proportion to their size, and capable of barking like European dogs. Fitzroy also noted this trait in the Fuegian Dogs that he observed in the 1830s. Members of the Cook Expedition noted this trait when they visited the southeast end of Tierra del Fuego in 1769. They observed dogs "about two feet high with sharp ears" that barked furiously. Cook's report is the earliest evidence concerning Fuegian Dogs and is in agreement with observations up to 1900.

In overall appearance, the Fuegian Dog is judged by Allen to be very similar to the Small Indian Dog, and the Techichi or Alco of Peru and Mexico. A look at the different uses of the two would cause a greater attraction to the dog of the harsh southern islands since it was a true aid to man while the other served only for food and play.

And companions they were, traveling always with the family groups in their dugout canoes. Captain King described in his journal how they were "met by three canoes, containing together, about twenty people, and ten or twelve dogs." The canoes were only about ten feet long and had three compartments. The third was usually occupied by the elder children and the dogs. Small size is typical of dogs that are owned by canoe traveling Indians, and so it was with the Fuegian Dog of the Ona, Yahgan, and Alacaluf Indians. Bred over the past hundreds of years, this dog of webbed feet and strong shoulders, deep chest and light frame for swimming, and a keen sense of purpose in and under water is surely the most unique of all Indian Dogs. "Miserable," as described by Darwin, these people may have been, but they were wise in the ways of survival and experts in training their dogs—these most hardy of all the American Indians.

Sketch of a Fuegian Dog brought to France in 1883.

War dogs being brought to Central America and the Caribbean Islands by Columbus' Second Expedition. (Woodcut by J. A. Loucier, 1582.)

War Dogs from Europe

The second great importation of dogs to America, this time from European lands rather than northeastern Asia, began with the voyages of Christopher Columbus. The bringing of dogs on the voyages across the Atlantic Ocean continued with almost every explorer. It was a certainty on every ship that brought the later immigrants to the American shores.

These earliest adventurers from Europe had a devastating impact on the Indian population. They brought diseases, foreign values, and war! The impact of European dogs on the native canine population was just as devastating. The magnitude of the disastrous effects can be measured by the rapid decline of the native populations. For instance, in the West Indies, within fifty years after their discovery by Columbus, the Taino Indian population was almost totally eliminated. Only a few hundred Indians remained out of an initial population of about one-quarter million. The large Indian dog population was almost totally eliminated. The fate of the dogs was slaughter for food and, as their masters were defeated, abandonment to the wilds.

It was an almost unvarying chain of events that preceded the Indians' defeat. Their initial wonder on first meeting the white man was followed by a short period of mutual respect. The giving of help in exchange for trade goods bound together the Indians and the explorers. Soon the need for land and the shooting of game for food by the Europeans offended the natives. Wherever the always-hoped-for presence of gold or silver materialized, harshest of relationships soon followed. Almost without exception, slavery, treachery, and killing became the bases for existence until the final defeat of the Indians. This pattern of events occurred over and over again during the three hundred years that followed the discovery of the New World by Columbus.

Of course, the Indians were usually at a disadvantage in dealings with the wily and purposeful Europeans. Their system of values based on living in harmony with nature was unable to control the foreign invaders. Nor were the Indians equal in war to the Europeans. At the time of Columbus, war tactics in Europe were the result of three hundred years of prior advances. Superior weapons and armor were based on the science of metals and machinery. The disciplined troops had replaced unruly brigades. The maneuvering and supporting in the field of large groups of soldiers was developed to a high art. Even the skills of the animal breeder were turned to aid the military. Finely bred and well trained horses and large war dogs were parts of every army. Gunpowder, steel, the horse, and ferocious dogs were all new to the Indian. All the then-modern military arts and skills were used in the conquest of the Indian nations that were encountered by the Europeans.

The first meetings in 1492 between Columbus and the Taino Indians produced the usual wonder and guarded respect. The natives were tremendously pleased with the Admiral's gifts of red caps, glass beads, and hawk's bells. Columbus was impressed with the Indians' guilelessness and generosity. Of these children of nature, Columbus wrote, "They invite you to share anything that they possess and show as much love as if their hearts went with it!" But Columbus, except at the site at Navidad, made no attempt during his first voyage to start settlements or engage in the search for gold. As a result, peace and civil relations were maintained with the Indians at his many stops in the Bahamas and on Cuba and Hispaniola. He was even able to persuade a few male Indians to accompany him back to Spain in February 1493.

The saga of relations between white men and Indians took its usual course shortly after Columbus' second arrival in the West Indies. The behavior of the twenty-one men left at Navidad had brought forth the usual form of Indian retribution--all twenty-one were killed. The small settlement at Navidad was the result of a chance grounding of the ship Santa Maria off the coast of Hispaniola. With limited space on the remaining Nina and Pinta, the excess crewmen were left behind to await the coming of ships the next year. When Columbus returned in November the following year, he was amply prepared as Admiral of a fleet of seventeen vessels. This great Spanish expedition across the Atlantic included twelve hundred seamen, colonists, and men-at-arms.

Some initial skirmishes were fought by Columbus and his men during the last few months of exploration in 1493. The first record of a war-like engagement appears in *The Decades of the New World of West Indies* that was written in 1515 by Peter Martyr, d'Angliera. This friend of Columbus describes the May 5, 1494, fight near Rio Bueno, Jamaica.

Carried in the seventeen vessels of the Second Expedition were purebred Spanish hounds, pointers, and mastiffs. (See page 168.) Other groups of dogs arrived at regular intervals as new ships from Spain landed at the trading town of Isabella. The first use of a large war dog was at Rio Bueno, where the natives began hostile demonstrations. Sixty or seventy Indian warriors came out in dugout canoes to meet the fleet and showed signs of giving fight. Columbus attacked from his ship's boats, and drove them to shore with a deluge of arrows shot by men with crossbows. They "pricked them well and killed a number." He then landed his troops and set upon them a great dog that "bit them and did them great hurt, for a dog is worth ten men against Indians." So said Peter Martyr. Although the use of dogs to attack Indians may have occurred during Columbus' earlier explorations, this event on Jamaica is the first to be reported by an authority. It is a unique occurrence—the first time an American was bitten by a European dog!

More purposeful attacks by dogs, led by organized Spanish men-at-arms, occurred later in 1495 on the Isle of Hispaniola, now the Dominican Republic. These attacks are shown vividly in scenes from Antonio de Herrera's *Historia* of 1601. This work describes Columbus' voyages to the West Indies. On the title page of the book are sketches that depict important events at Navidad. Included are two scenes of natives with bows and arrows engaged in combat with Spanish warriors in armor, on horseback, and with fierce war dogs. It is reported that these first pitched battles between Spaniards and Indians, shown in the scenes on page 173, took place at the end of March 1495. The tactics of worrying Indians with big, savage dogs were not devised for the New World, for they had been used earlier on the Indians of the Canary Islands. The Indian Chief Guatiguana tried to unite the Indians of Hispaniola to resist the Spanish. He collected a formidable army, estimated in the thousands, to march on the town of Isabella which had just been established by Columbus. The Spanish took the offensive and, led by Columbus, marched to Puerto de los Hidalgos with twenty horses, ten hounds, and two hundred foot soldiers, half of them armed with arquebuses. The gunfire from these primitive weapons could only alarm the Tainos Indians, but when the cavalry charged and the savage dogs were unleashed to attack, the rout of the Indians was complete.

Within ten years after their discovery, the West Indian natives were totally subjugated, virtual slaves of the Spanish. During this period, more than two hundred ships had sailed westward for the Indies. Thousands of seamen and settlers had left for the New World to seek riches, trade, and land. During this period, Columbus and other daring sea captains continued the explorations of the western islands and the lands bordering the Gulf of Mexico. Dogs were in abundance. They were fine companions during the long sea voyages and in strange lands. They were frequent passengers on the ships, giving comfort both to ships officers and ordinary seamen. When on land they served other purposes.

171

One of the more important was official taster to determine whether foods were poisonous. It was common for workers to fall ill of malaria or from drinking well water and eating strange fish. To guard against sickness, Dr. Chanca, Columbus' fleet surgeon, tried every new type of food on a dog before he would let any Christian try it. Surely this is the first use of dogs for medical research in the New World and to protect the lives of humans.

Among the many dogs carried to the West Indies during the four voyages of the Admiral of the Ocean Sea, one or more must have been Columbus' favorite. Then again, he may have been too busy or too strong of will during his early voyages to recognize the pleasure of having a friendly dog at his side. For it was only during his last expedition, which began in 1502, when Columbus was fifty-one years old, that he reports the presence of a pet dog. It was on this voyage that he discovered the lands that are now Honduras, Nicaragua, Costa Rica, Panama, and Colombia.

While reconnoitering along the east coast of Costa Rica, Columbus sent an armed party into the country in search of game. They met the Indians of Puerto Limon who presented them with two wild pigs. One they kept and brought on board ship. Columbus reports in his diary that it was so fierce and aggressive that his Irish Wolfhound remained below decks as long as the porker was on board. This dog must have been a favorite of Columbus since it is the only dog that he tells about in all his reports of these voyages.

The dog was still with Columbus a half year later when it was decided to establish a trading site at the mouth of the Rio Belen on the coast of Panama. On April 6, 1503, while farewells were being said on board ship in the harbor, the fort was attacked by hundreds of Indians. The small garrison of twenty men there, at this time, would easily have been overrun except for the presence of the Irish Wolfhound. Columbus reports that, fortunately, he had decided to leave his dog to help guard the fort. He states proudly how the Indians with bows and arrows and spears were beaten off, largely through the rough work of his pet hound.

These two tales of a dog used as a companion and to attack outsiders show the actions of a trained animal. These large dogs were docile creatures when among their Spanish friends and masters but turned into savage beasts when ordered to attack the helpless Indians. It is noted in some of the earliest of reports that the dogs of Spain had a particular aversion to the smell of Indians and would attack with but little encouragement. From the many reports of the period, one is bound to accept this statement as true.

172

Scenes of Columbus' 1495
attack with war dogs on the
Caciques of Hispaniola. From
a 1601 Spanish history of
Columbus' voyages to the
West Indies.

173

During the famous crossing of Panama in September 1513 by Vasco Nunez de Balboa and his entourage of about two hundred Spaniards and several hundred native guides and porters, they engaged in a fight with the army of a local chieftain. Balboa captured about forty members of the chief's male harem, homosexuality being a not uncommon practice of native tribes that lived in the tropics. Since it was deemed a cardinal sin by the Spanish to engage in "the infamous practice," Balboa took the strongest measures against the men whenever it was encountered. In this instance, he set his dogs upon them and "had them torn apart." The scene of this horrible, but rather commonplace, event was depicted by the artist Theodor De Brey in his book written in 1540 and is shown on page 177. Like other Christians of the era, Balboa had no compassion for sodomites. This attitude explains the casual stance of the Spanish conquistadors in the horrible scene of human mutilation by a pack of savage dogs!

One of the dogs in the De Brey scene may have been the dog Leoncille, or Leonzico, a "red bloodhound with black nose and eyes" owned by Balboa. According to Oviedo, a biographer of Balboa, Leoncille had "gained for his master more than two thousand pesos in gold." In the conquest of the New World, it was common for the Spaniards to show their admiration for a good fighting dog by giving him a part of their winnings, or rather by leaving the dog's portion to his master, who as a result received a share and one-half of the amount due a man of his profession. It is reported by Garcilaso de la Vega that "Leoncille received 100 pesos in gold as his share in one of the divisions made after Balboa had discovered the Sea of the South (the Pacific)."

Leoncille was a male pup of Becerrillo or Bezerrico, who belonged to Ponce de Leon, no doubt the result of some special breeding program, for Becerrillo was said to have been able to distinguish between a peaceful Indian and a warrior. This ability of a well-bred Spanish dog in the New World is told by Vega about a Greyhound that had witnessed the sudden flight of four Indian captives.

The Indians ate in complete tranquility, but when the Castilians were feeling most carefree about them, all four arose simultaneously and raced as fast as they could to the forest. In fact, they traveled so swiftly that the Christians doubted their ability to overtake them on foot, and they were unable to ride after since the horses were not at hand. Meanwhile, however, a greyhound chanced to be close by, and on hearing the Spaniards shout to the Indians and seeing the latter in flight, he set out in pursuit. Then just as if possessed of human

174

understanding, this dog rushed by the first three Indians he came to and on reaching the fourth, who was in advance of the others, threw a paw to his shoulder and knocked him to the ground, holding him there until the next man approached. And now as each successive Indian came near and attempted to pass, the animal released the one he was holding and tossed another to the ground. And when he had thrown the last, he went back and forth among the four of them with such skill and trickery, turning loose one to hurl down another who was attempting to rise and frightening them all with great barks as he lay his paw upon them, that he was able to detain them until the Spaniards arrived and took them back to the camp.

This revered and feared Greyhound was known as Bruto. Vega also reported that:

The Spaniards were talking peacefully one day with some natives on the bank of a river in another province when a bold Indian, such as many of them are, struck a Spaniard viciously with his bow, for no reason whatsoever, and then plunged into the water, followed by his companions. Being nearby, this same greyhound Bruto witnessed the deed and darted after the Indians. Some of them he soon overtook, but he did not seize a single one until he came to the individual who had delivered the blow. Then striking this man with his paw, he proceeded to tear him to pieces in the water.

In addition to his other offenses against the natives, Bruto had guarded the army at night so that no hostile Indian could enter the camp without being destroyed at once. Hence, as I have said, the Indians now avenged themselves against this greyhound by taking his life. For having identified him by rumor, they shot at him most eagerly, and in doing so revealed their skill in the use of the bow and arrow.

Bruto was a savage Greyhound in the service of Hernando de Soto during his conquest of Florida. The Greyhound was a favored breed among the Spanish on this expedition. All the descriptions in the Vega report of this 1539, seven-ship expedition to the coast bordering the Gulf of Mexico relate to Greyhounds. During the passage from Cuba Vega reported that:

There was in our company an hidalgo named Tapia, a native of Arevalo. This man had with him a very fine and valuable greyhound

175

which also fell overboard when we were something like twelve leagues from port. As a fair wind was blowing, we could not stop to rescue the animal and consequently left it in the sea while we continued on our way into port. The following morning, Tapia, very much to his surprise and happiness, beheld his dog on land and attempted to regain it; but the man who now had possession of the animal prevented his doing so. It was found to be true that this greyhound, after falling into the sea, had swum for five hours before being discovered and brought aboard a vessel that was cruising among the islands.

On another occasion along the Ocali River in Florida, Vega relates how a particular Greyhound gave chase to some renegade Indians—and was killed in the process because of his eagerness. The incident came about during an inspection by Balboa and Chief Ocali of a site for the location of a bridge since it was deemed necessary that one be constructed before the river could be crossed.

One day he and the Curaca went out to see where the structure could be located, and as they were strolling along and planning the bridge, more than five hundred native archers rushed out from the bushes growing on the opposite bank and shouted: "So you thieves, vagabonds, and foreign immigrants want a bridge. You will not see it built with our hands." And with these taunts they cast a sprinkling of arrows toward where the Governor and the Cacique Ocali stood.

On firing their arrows the Indians had raised a shout which provoked a greyhound to dash forward. Dragging to the ground one of the Governor's pages who was holding it by the collar, the dog now freed itself and plunged into the water, refusing to return in spite of the repeated commands of its masters. Then as the animal swam the stream the Indians hurled their arrows so skillfully that more than fifty of them penetrated its head and shoulders, which were above the water. Even so, the dog succeeded in reaching land, only to fall dead immediately on leaving the water. The Governor and all of his companions were much grieved at the loss of this particular greyhound, for it was a rare hunter and very necessary for the conquest. Within the short span of its life, it had made skillful and admirable attacks on the Indians both by day and by night.

While incursions into the Americas of foreigners and their dogs from different European countries occurred at many times during the next two hundred years, the ensuing events were always the same. After the initial friendly greetings, the Indian warriors were eliminated and their remaining members retreated. During these encounters, as noted by Vega and others, the European dogs typically were killed in combat or died through hard use and accidents. No attempts had to be made to preserve them since an abundant supply existed. They could be replaced easily during the next sailing.

Since they were used principally for war or the tracking of the Indians, they were feared and hated by the natives who would have had no desire to own them or use them for breeding. Even chance breedings would have had little lasting impact because of the overwhelming number of Indian dogs that continued to propagate. Up to the late 1700s, the seventeen identifiable breeds of Indian dogs remained indigenous to each tribal group, uncorrupted by imported European canine cousins.

The killing of Indians by war dogs of Balboa during the crossing of Panama on the way to the Pacific. (By Theodor De Brey, 1540.)

177

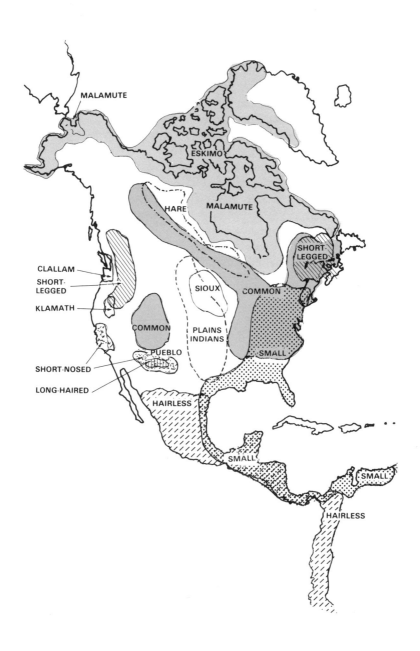

Approximate areas of North and Central America where various
breeds of Indian Dogs were to be found.

178

Tale's End

It is clear from the ample evidence already presented in pictures and discussions that a dog culture existed among most Indians for many thousands of years prior to the coming of the white man. Of the twenty million or more Indians that lived in the Americas, almost all had dogs in abundance. Only a few tribes considered the dog an unwelcome partner and lived without the benefits that were a part of most associations with *canis familiaris*. Their uses were many and in some areas they were absolutely essential for survival of the tribal family groups. Although their number varied depending on local conditions, it appears that they too could be counted in the tens of millions. We know that they were most populous among the Eskimo and Plains Indians, numbering about four times the native population. For the Woodland Indians and tribes of the mountain areas, one or two dogs for each family group was usual. While small areas in North America were without dogs, such as portions of Central California, there were vast regions of tropical South America that never heard the bark of a dog.

Writing about Brazil after his sojourn along the coast in 1500, Amerigo Vespucci described the wealth of animals as "so many that it would have been hard for them to enter Noah's ark . . . but no domesticated animals whatsoever, they do not have."

Considering their variation in number among each of the Indian cultural groups, and the size of the native populations, it is reasonable to figure the Indian dog population at the height of development in the Americas as about sixty million. Their distribution by breed over the land areas is shown for North and Central America on page 178 and for South America on page 158. Almost all the inhabited areas of North America had one or more distinctly different breed of dogs.

The map on page 180 shows in detail particular aspects of the dog culture in the area of the far western United States. The information was gathered by A. L. Kroeber from reports in this region of Indian activities related to canids prior to 1900. We know that the Clallam-Indian Dogs provided the textile use indicated in the figure. While the Common and Short-nosed Indian Dogs were present over large areas of the West, the

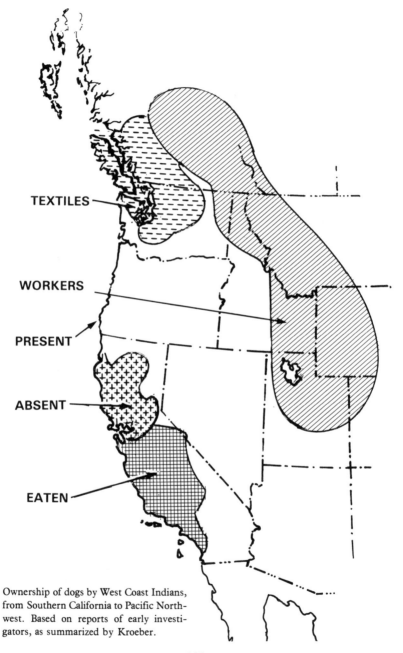

TEXTILES

WORKERS

PRESENT

ABSENT

EATEN

Ownership of dogs by West Coast Indians,
from Southern California to Pacific Northwest. Based on reports of early investigators, as summarized by Kroeber.

almost total absence of dogs north and east of the San Francisco Bay area is a unique condition. One can accept the Brazilian lack of dogs as the result of the ecosystem, characterized by abundant food, mild climate, water transport, and deadly predators. All these conditions make the presence of dogs either unnecessary or impossible to sustain. In California, the first two of these conditions—mild climate and abundant food—prevailed and may account for the lack of interest in breeding dogs. Why bother with dogs when life is so comfortable and there is no need to be moving over great distances in search of food. Even the warmth gained from contact with one's dog would be unnecessary in the mild climates of California and Brazil.

With these two exceptions, dogs were needed as aides and comforters in daily life in all other tribal areas. Each period in the life of the Indian had important moments with dogs. By the time the Indian child crawled from the wigwam or family hut, the fondling of soft and tender puppies was a common occurrence. The happiness of an Indian child with pups is most evident in a reproduction of a photograph that was taken by Rodman Wanamaker during the last gathering of the remaining Indian Chiefs in 1909. (Page 182.) This very special event in the long history of the American Indian was recorded by Dr. Joseph K. Dixon in the book *The Vanishing Race, The Last Great Indian Council.* The sixteen Indian chiefs, representing the main remaining Indian tribes in the United States, along with five renowned scouts of General Custer, were assembled with their families in the Valley of the Little Big Horn in Montana.

This last council was conceived by Wanamaker and Dixon, and was supported by the Bureau of Indian Affairs and the Indian superintendents on the various reservations. The most distinguished chiefs, eminent for ability and achievement, were invited along with interpreters, to participate in this emotionally powerful gathering. The event involved the construction of a primitive council lodge along with an array of shining tepees and native paraphernalia. Dixon, in his record of the council, notes that "Months of arduous labor were spent in the effort to make a comprehensive and permanent record of an old-time Indian council." Special care was taken to provide a friendly setting for all who came to the council in order to remove the natural reserve of the Indians so that the Chiefs would reveal their inner selves. Encouraged by all, each in turn had the opportunity to speak in his native language about his Indian world and about what he thought and how he felt. They met in solemn conclave to hold communion and to say a long and last farewell. They spoke of youthful exploits and savage warfare with the white man.

There could be no greater joy for the young Indian child than to fondle warm and loving pups. This photograph, entitled "Little Friends," was taken by Rodman Wanamaker in 1913 during the Last Great Indian Council.

182

They described their weapons and the hallowed sites of old. They spoke of governing the tribes—and of the wild chase of the hunter—and about their Indian dogs.

Even in the camp of thirty tepees of this last council, every Indian family took pride in the ownership of a number of dogs. In the camp, it was estimated that there were over three hundred dogs. They had free run of the lodges and at night slept by their Indian masters in the tepees. During the days, the noisy, gleeful group of children that accompanied the chiefs and scouts played with their dolls and dogs—dogs that were used by the children as playthings, beasts of burden, or to ride and to torment and to torture. The youthful life among the Crow Indians was described by White-Man-Run-Him, Chief of the Custer scouts, and included exploits with dogs. This eminent Crow was sixty-five at the time of the council and described his boyhood as follows:

Until I was fifteen years of age, together with my boy playmates, we trained with bows and arrows. We learned to shoot buffalo calves, and this practice gave us training for the warpath.... We were also taught the management of horses. We early learned how to ride well....We felt brave enough to meet anything. Thus it was that we roamed over the hills, and climbed the rocks in search of game. If on our way to the new camp we came across game, such as a rabbit, we shot it with our arrows, boiled it and ate it for fun.... The little girls had small tepees. They practised working, learning from the older women. These girls would serve delicacies to us, and we would sing and dance around their tepees .... When we were quite small boys we would go out hunting horses, and bring back a dog and call it a horse .... We were surrounded by many different tribes, Shoshones, Sioux, Piegans and Gros Ventres. They were all our enemies. We often went on the warpath against these people, because they were always trying to take our horses and conquer our land .... Going back to the days when we had no horses, we would see the buffalo on the plains; we then surrounded them, driving them as we did so, near to the edge of some steep precipice .... We would play with dogs, making believe that they were buffalo and try to surround them .... The Indians found some dogs on the prairie. After they got the dogs they would fasten a pole on either side of the dogs with a tanned hide fastened between the poles, and the Indian would put their trappings, their meat, and their papooses on this hide stretched between the poles. In that way they moved from place to place, the dog carrying the utensils of the camp .... One day when we were moving, the dog who was carrying a baby

Crow warrior and dogs photographed about 1906 by Edward S. Curtis.

184

in the travois saw a deer and ran after it. He went over a bank and carried the baby with him, and finally came back without the baby.

Even as a lonely old man, this Crow warrior had vivid memories of dogs on the prairie as objects of enjoyment, as workers, and as the cause of great pain to an Indian family. Whether hauling a sled, pulling a travois, or backpacking (as seen on page 184, the reproduction of a photograph taken by Edward S. Curtis about 1906), the Indian dog was a worker. Anguish and pain he also caused by his erratic behavior. Finally, the Indian dog was held by many as a sacrificial object. The death scene below depicts the actions of an Indian shaman, and conveys the ultimate role of the dog—to be killed to guard his master in the afterworld or to appease the spirits.

The sacrifice of prized dogs during a tribal ritual was common practice among some Indians.

References

Allen, Glover M. "Dogs of the American Aborigines." *Bulletin of the Museum of Comparative Zoology.* Harvard College, Vol. 43, No. 9, Cambridge, Mass. March, 1920.

Barton, B. S. "Some Accounts of the Different Species and Varieties of Native American, or Indian Dogs." *Bartons Medical and Physiological Journal,* I, pt. 2, pp. 3-31, Philadelphia. 1795.

Beebe, B. F. "A Domestic Dog (Canine Familiaris L.) of Probable Pleistocene Age From Old Crow, Yukon Territory, Canada." *Canadian Journal of Archaeology,* No. 4. 1980.

Brisbin, Jr., I. Lehr. "The Domestication of the Dog." *Pure-Bred Dogs American Kennel Gazette.* January, 1976.

Brisbin, Jr., I. Lehr. "The Pariah." *Pure-Bred Dogs American Kennel Gazette.* January, 1977.

Butler, Eva M., and Hadlock, Wendell S. "Dogs of the Northeastern Woodland Indians." *Mass. Archaeological Society Bulletin,* Vol. 10, No. 2, pp. 17-35. 1949.

Canby, Thomas Y. "The Search for the First Americans." *National Geographic,* 2 pp. 330-363. 1979.

Cartwright, George. Journal of the Transactions and Events During A Residence of Nearly 16 Years On the Coast of Labrador, Vol. 1. Ams. Press. 1793. Reprinted 1930.

Clutton-Brock, Juliet. "Man-Made Dogs." *Science,* Vol. 197, pp. 1340-1342. 1977.

Colton, Harold S. "The Aboriginal Southwestern Indian Dog." *American Antiquity,* Vol. 35, No. 2. 1970.

Coronado, Francisco Vasquez de. *The Journey of Coronado, 1540-1542.* Edited by George P. Winship. New York. 1922.

Coues, Elliott, ed., "New Light on the Early History of the Greater Northwest." *The Henry-Thompson Journals.* New York. 1897.

Davis, Simon J. M., and Valla, Francois R. "Evidence for Domestication of the Dog 12,000 Years Ago in the Natufian of Israel." *Nature,* Vol. 276, pp. 608-610. 1978.

Degerbol, Magnus. "On a Find of a Preboreal Domestic Dog From Star Carr, Yorkshire, with Remarks on Other Mesolithic Dogs." *The Prehistoric Society,* No. 3, pp. 35-55. 1961.

Denys, N. *Descriptions and Natural History of the Coasts of North America.* Edited by W. F. Ganong. Publications of the Champlain Society, Vol. 2. 1908.

Elvas. "True Relation of the Hardships Suffered by Governor Fernando de Soto . . . by a Gentleman of Elvas." 2 vol. Edited and translated by Alexander Robertson. 1932-33.

Emslie, Steven D. "Dog Burials From Mancos Canyon, Colorado." *The Kiva,* Vol. 43, No. 3-4. 1978.

Galbreath, Edwin C. "Post-Glacial Fossil Vertebrates from East-Central Illinois." Geological Series of Field Museum of Natural History, Vol. 6 (20), pp. 303-313. 1938.

Grant, Campbell; Baird, James W.; and Pringle, J. Kenneth. *Rock Drawings of the Caso Range.* Maturango Press, Maturango, California. 1968.

Grant, Campbell. *Rock Art of the American Indian.* Promontory Press, New York. 1967.

Guernsey, S. J., and Kidder, A. V. "Basket-Maker Caves of N.E. Arizona." Peabody Museum, Cambridge. 1921.

Haag, Wm. G. "An Osteometric Analysis of Some Aboriginal Dogs." *Reports in Anthropology.* University of Kentucky, Lexington, Kentucky, Vol. 7, pp. 107-263. 1948.

Hammond, George P., and Rey, Agapito. "The Rodriguez Expedition to New Mexico, 1581-1582." *New Mexico Historical Review,* II. October, 1927.

Haury, Emil W. *The Stratigraphy and Archaeology of Ventana Cave.* University of Arizona Press, Tucson, Arizona. 1975.

Haynes, Jr., C. Vance. "Elephant Hunting in North America." *Scientific American,* Vol. 214 (6), pp. 104-112. 1960.

Haynes, Jr., C. Vance. "The Earliest Americans." *Science,* pp. 709-715. 1969.

Healy, Michael A. *Report of the Cruise of the Revenue Marine Steamer Corwin in the Arctic Ocean in the Year 1885.* Washington, D.C., Government Printing Office. 1887.

Healy, Michael A. *Report of the Cruise of the Revenue Marine Steamer Corwin in the Arctic Ocean in the Year 1884.* Washington, D.C., Government Printing Office. 1889.

Herculais, J. K. d'. "Les Chiens des Fuegiens." *Science et Nature,* 1, sem. 1, pp. 137-140. 1884.

Hill, Frederick. C. *A Middle Archaic Dog Burial in Illinois.* Foundation of Illinois Archaeology, Evanston, Ill. 1972.

Irving, W. N., and Harington, C. R. "Upper Pleistocene Radiocarbon-Dated Artifacts from the Northern Yukon." *Science,* Vol. 179 (4071), pp. 335-340. 1973.

Ives, S., and Barry, R., eds. *Arctic and Alpine Environments.* Paleolithic Players on the American State: Man's Impact on the Late Pleistocene Megafauna, pp. 669-700. 1975.

Josephy, Alvin M. *The Artist Was A Young Man, The Life Story of Peter Rindisbacher.* Amon Carter Museum, Forth Worth. 1970.

Kane, Elisha K. Arctic Explorations, 2 V. Phila.: Childs and Peterson. 1856.

Kroeber, A. L. "Culture Element Distributions: XV, Salt, Dogs, Tobacco." *Anthropological Records.* University of California. 1941.

La Verendrye. *Journals and Letters of Pierre Gaultier de Varennes, Sieur de la Verendrye, and His Sons.* Edited by Lawrence J. Burpee. Toronto. 1927.

Larsen, Hillge. "Trail Creek, Final Report on the Excavation of two Caves on Seward Peninsula, Alaska." Acta Artica, Fasc. 15, 79 pages + 8 pl. 1968.

Lawrence, Barbara. "Early Domestic Dogs." *Zeitschrift Fur Saugetierkundle,* 32 Band, pp. 44-59. 1967.

Lawrence, Barbara. "Antiquity of Large Dogs in North America." *Tebiwa,* Vol. 11 (2), pp. 42-49. 1968.

Lawrence, Barbara, and Bossert, William H. "Multiple Character Analysis of Canis lupus, latrans and familiaris, with a Discussion of the Relationship of Canis niger." *Am. Geologist,* Vol. 7, pp. 223-232. 1967.

Leach, Maria. *God Had a Dog.* Rutgers University Press, New Brunswick, N.J., 1961.

Lyon, George F. *The Private Narrative of An Unsuccessful Attempt to Reach Repulse Bay.* London, John Murray. 1824.

MacNeish, Richard S. "Early Man In the Andes." *Scientific American,* Vol. 224 (4), pp. 36-46.

Mallery, Garrick. *Pictographs of the North American Indians.* Fourth Annual Report of the Bureau of American Ethnology. Washington, D.C. 1886.

Mallery, Garrick. *Picture Writing of the American Indians.* Tenth Annual Report of the Bureau of American Ethnology. Washington, D.C. 1893.

Martin, Paul S. "The Discovery of America." *Science,* Vol. 179, pp. 969-974. 1973.

Martin, Paul S. "Palaeolithic Players on the American Stage: Man's Impact on the Late Pleistocene Megafauna." Chapter 11, *Arctic and Alpine Environments.* Edited by S. Ives and E. Barry. Methuen Co., London. 1975.

Martin, Paul S., and Wright, Jr., H. E., eds. "The Search for a Cause." *Pleistocene Extinctions.* Yale University Press, New Haven & London. 1967.

McMillan, R. Bruce. "Early Canid Burial from the Western Ozark Highland." *Science,* Vol. 167, pp. 1246-1247. 1970.

Mech, L. David. *The Wolf: The Ecology and Behavior of an Endangered Species.* The Natural History Press. Garden City, N.Y. 1972.

Miller, Carl F. "Life Uncovered 8000 Years Ago in an Alabama Cave." *National Geography,* Vol. CX #4, pp. 542-558. October, 1956.

Miller, Malcolm E. *Anatomy of the Dog.* W. B. Saunders Company, Philadelphia, Pa. 1964.

Moore, George T., and Theresa M. "Tracing the Canine Ancestry." *Pure-Bred Dogs American Kennel Gazette.* Aug., 1979.

Muller-Beck, Hansjurgen, "Paleohunters in America, Origins and Diffusion." *Science,* Vol. 152 (3726), pp. 1191-1210. 1966.

Mosimann, James E., and Martin, Paul S. "Simulating Overkill by Paleo-Indians." *American Scientist,* 63 (3), pp. 304-313. 1975.

Olsen, Stanley J. "Early Domestic Dogs in North America and Their Origins." *Journal of Field Archaeology,* Vol. 1, pp. 343-345. 1974.

Olsen, Stanley J., and Olsen, John W. "The Chinese Wolf, Ancestor of New World Dogs." *Science,* Vol. 197, pp. 533-535. 1977.

Oswalt, W. H. *Eskimos and Explorers.* Chandler Sharp Publishers, Novato, Calif. 1979.

Oviedo y Valdes, G.F. *General and Natural History of the Indies.* 1535. (Reprint, Madrid, 4 Vols., 1851-55.)

Parry, William E. *Journal of Second Voyage for the Discovery of a Northwest Passage.* London, John Murray. 1824.

Recchi, N. A., and Lynceus, J. T. *Rerum Medicarum Novae Hispaniae Thesaurus seu Plantarum, Animalium, Mineralium Mexicanorum Historia ex Francisco Hernandez.* Rome. 1651.

Richardson, Sir John. *Fauna Boreali-Americana.* 4 vols. London. 1829-1837.

Ritchie, William A. "The Lamoka Lake Site." Researches and Transactions of the New York State Archaeology Association, Vol. 7 (4), pp. 79-134. 1932.

Ritchie, William A. *The Archaeology of Martha's Vineyard.* Natural History Press, Garden City, N.Y. 1969.

Ritchie, William A. *The Archaeology of New York State.* Natural History Press, Garden City, N.Y. 1974.

Roe, F. G. *The Indian And The Horse.* University of Oklahoma Press, Norman, Oklahoma. 19-.

Roe, F. G. "From Dogs to Horses Among the Western Indian Tribes." Proceedings and Transactions of the Royal Society of Canada, Vol. 33. 1939.

Ross, John A. *Voyage of Discovery.* London: John Murray. 1819.

Scott, L. G., and Middleton, J. *The Labrador Dog, Its Home and History.* Witherley, London. 1936.

Shetrone, Henry C. *The Mound Builders.* D. Appelton and Co., New York. 1930.

Scott, J. P. "Evolution and Domestication of the Dog." *Evolutionary Biology.* 1968.

Simpson, John. *"The Western Eskimo."* On: A Selection of Papers on Arctic Geography and Ethnology. John Murray. London. 1875.

Speck, F. G. "Dogs of the Labrador Indians." *Natural History,* Vol. 25, #1. N.J. 1925.

Stoctdale, A. "The Hairless Dog." *Journal of Heredity,* pp. 519-520. 1917.

Struever, Stuart, and Holton, Felicia Antonelli. *Koster, Americans in Search of Their Prehistoric Past.* Anchor Press/Doubleday, Garden City, New York. 1979.

Tuck, James A. "An Archaic Indian Cemetery in Newfoundland." *Scientific American,* pp. 113-120. 1970.

Webb, Wm. S. "The Carlson Annis Mound." *Reports in Anthropology*, Vol 7 (4), pp. 267-295. 1950.

Webb, Wm. S. "The Read Shell Midden." *Reports in Anthropology*, Vol. 7 (5), pp. 357-390. 1950.

Wheat, Joe Ben. "A Paleo-Indian Bison Kill." *Scientific American,* 216 (1), pp. 44-52.

Wilson, G. L. "The Horse and The Dog in Hidatsa Culture." *Anthropological Papers of the American Museum of Natural History,* Vol. 15. 1924.

Wood, W. Raymond, and McMillan, R. Bruce. "Recent Investigations at Rodgers Shelter, Missouri." *Archaeology,* Vol. 20 #1, pp. 52-55. January 1967.

Young, Stanley P. "What Was The Early Indian Dog?" *American Forests.* December, 1943. January, 1944.

Zagoskin, Laurentiy A. "Lieutenant Zagoskin's Travels in Russian America, 1842-1844." Edited by Henry N. Michael. Arctic Institute of North America, Anthropology of the North: Translations from Russian Sources. Nov. 7, 1967.

Index

Alexander Philip Maximilian, 82, 88, 90
Allen, Dr. Glover M., 64, 66, 76, 88, 116, 123, 125, 128, 138, 143–144, 146, 147–149, 154, 156, 159, 167
Allen, Dr. J. A., 144, 145
Asdell, Dr. S. A., 75
Audubon, John James, 105
Audubon, John W., 119, 120

Bachman, Rev. John, 10, 105
Balboa, Vasco Nunez de, 174, 176
Barton, B. S., 130–131, 135
Baumhoff, M., 55
Beebe, Dr. Brenda F., 4, 25
Bercerrillo (Bezerrico), 174
Berczy, William, 136
Berners, Juliana, 11
Birch Creek Valley, Idaho, 46
Bodmer, Karl, 81, 82, 83, 86, 88, 92
Bossert, William H., 29, 33
Brant, Chief Joseph, 136
Bruto, 175
Bryon, 164–165
Buffalo-Bird-Woman, 81, 82, 90–91, 97, 138

Cabot, William P., 128
Caius, Dr. Johannes, 11
Cantwell, Lt. Jon C., 116
Castaneda, Pedro de, 79
Catlin, George, 80, 81, 83–84, 88, 90, 92, 94, 96–97
Chanca, Dr., 172
Clallam-Indian Dog, 139–140, 156, 157, 179
Clark, William, 80, 91
Clovis, New Mexico, 26
Colton, Dr. Harold S., 62, 64, 146
Columbus, Christopher, 10, 73, 129–130, 169–172
Common Indian Dog, 128–134, 154, 159, 162, 179
Cook Expedition, 166
Coronado, Francisco Vasquez de, 79–80, 147

Cortes, Hernando, 135
Cortes Hojia Expedition, 156
Corwin, Rev. Cutter, 116
coyote, 21, 26, 27, 29, 31, 33, 46, 91, 97, 144
Curtis, Edward S., 185
Custer, Gen. George A., 181, 183

d'Angliera, Peter Martyr, 170–171
Darwin, Charles, 156, 160, 162, 164, 165, 167
Davies, Thomas, 131
Davis, John, 101
Day, W., 136
De Brey, Theodor, 174
de Leon, Ponce, 174
Del Techo, 156
Denys, Nicholas, 131–132
de Soto, Hernando, 10, 11, 134–135, 175
d'Herculais, 166
Dingo, 22
Dixon, Dr. Joseph K., 181

Eaton, G. F., 153
Ely Cave Dog, 144
Emslie, Dr. Steven D., 64
Eskimo Dogs, 99–102, 104–105, 109–113, 149
Espejo, 80

Fells Cave, Southern Peru, 43
Fidalgo of Elvas, 135
Fitzroy, Capt. Robert, 160, 165, 166
fox, 21, 135
Franklin, Capt. Sir John, 88, 118
Frobisher, Master Martin, 100, 123
Frontenac Island, 51, 53
Fuegian Dog, 162, 164–167

Gass, Sgt., 80
Gebhard, D., 55
Geneva, New York, 51
Gibbs, George, 138

Giocueta, 156
Gonzalez, Miguel, 135
Gould, Felix, 51
Grant, Campbell, 55, 56
Great Basin, Coso Mountain Range, 55–56, 58
Guatiguana, Chief, 171
Guernsey, S. J., 64, 143, 146, 156

Haag, William G., 29, 46, 62, 146
Hakluyt, Richard, 100, 101, 123, 130
Haltane, Sweden, 60
Hare-Indian Dog, 118–120, 123
Harington, Dr. C. R., 40
Ha-wan-je-tah, 92, 94
Healy, Capt. Michael A., 116, 117
Heizer, R. F., 55
Hernandez, Francisco, 134, 149
Herrara, Antonia de, 171
Hill, Dr. Frederick C., 49, 66
Holmes, W. H., 56, 58
Horse Canyon, 56
Huades, Dr., 166
Hunter, John, 130

Inca Dog, 153–154, 159, 162
Itasca Bison Site, Minnesota, 46

jackal, 21, 27
Jaguar Cave, Idaho, 9, 25, 41, 43, 44–46, 48, 52, 66
Jarmo, Iraq, 64
Jefferson, Thomas, 80
Jones, H., 136

Kane, Paul, 81, 97, 139
Kennicott, Robert, 154
Kidder, A. V., 64, 146, 156
King, Capt. P. Parker, 165, 167
King, Philip, 160, 162
Klamath-Indian Dog, 136, 138
Koster Farm Dog, Illinois, 48–49, 66
Kroeber, A. L., 179
Kville Parish, Bohuslan, 60

Las Casas, Bartolome de, 130
La Verendrye, 80
Lawrence, Barbara, 29, 33, 45–46, 66
Le Jeune, 128, 133–134
Leoncille (Leonzico), 174
Lewis, Meriwether, 80, 91

Libby, Dr. Willard F., 34, 35, 36, 37
Livermore, S. T., 127, 128
London, Jack, 73
Long-haired Inca Dog, 153, 154, 156–157
Long-haired Pueblo Dog, 143, 145–148, 156
Loomis, F. F., 125
Lord, P., 40
Luers, Hans E., 36, 37
Lynceus, 149
Lyon, George F., 101–102, 104–105

Malamute, 115–118
Mallery, Col. Garrick, 55, 56
Mancos Canyon, 64
Martens, Conrad, 165
Martin, Donald, 58
Martin, Prof. Paul S., 43, 44
McMillan, R. B., 48
Meighan, C., 55
Mendoza, 147
Mexican Hairless Dog, 148–150
Mosimann, James E., 43
Muller-Beck, Dr. Hansjurgen, 22

Nehring, Alfred, 153, 156, 159
Norrick, Frank A., 4

Ocali, Chief, 176
Old Crow Basin/River, Yukon, 24–25, 39, 40, 41, 46
Olsen, John W., 10, 26, 27
Olsen, Stanley J., 9–10, 26, 27
Onate, Don Juan de, 147
Oviedo, Gonzalo Fernandez de, 129, 174
Oyala, Guraman Poma de, 154

Parry, William E., 112
Patagonian Dog, 160, 162
Peary, Adm. Robert E., 100, 105
Peruvian Pug-nosed Dog, 159–160
Petroglyph Canyon, 56
Pitkin, William, 132–133
Plains-Indian Dog, 79–84, 86, 146
Port au Choix Dog, Newfoundland, 49–53, 60, 66

Recchi, 149
Rees, Dr. Abraham, 127–128
Richardson, John, 101, 118–119, 120, 123, 126, 127, 128

Rindisbacher, Peter, 81, 84, 86, 119, 120
Rio San Juan, 56, 58, 60
Ritchie, Dr. William A., 51
Rodgers Shelter Site, Missouri, 48, 49, 53
Roe, Frank Gilbert, 81
Ross, John, 102

Sackhouse, John, 102
Sadek-Kooros, Dr. Hind, 9, 44
Sanford, Maj., 94
Scott, D., 55
Seler, E., 150
Settle, Dionyse, 100
Sheep Canyon, 56
Short-legged Indian Dog, 125–128
Short-nosed Indian Dog, 143–145, 146, 159, 179
Sioux Dogs, 86, 88, 90–92, 94, 96–97
Small Indian Dog, 134–136, 167
Smith, C. Hamilton, 90, 140, 160, 165
Stefansson, Vilhjalmur, 105, 109, 110, 111–112
Stockdale, Arthur, 149, 150
Stoney, Naval Off. George M., 116
Struever, Dr. Stuart, 48
Suckley, George, 126, 127, 128, 138, 140

Tchan-dee, 92
Techichi, 134, 167
Thompson, D., 91–92
Tlatilco, Mexico, 64, 66
Trail Creek, Alaska, 25, 46

Tuck, James A., 51, 52, 66

Uncas, Ben, 132, 133

Valseguillo, Mexico, 64
Vancouver, George, 139–140
Vega, Garcilaso de la, 135, 174–176, 177
Vespucci, Amerigo, 179
von Ihering, Herman, 162
von Tschudi, J. J., 150

Wanamaker, Rodman, 181
White, A., 91–92
White Cave Dog, 143, 144, 145, 146, 147
White, John, 101
White-Man-Run-Him, Chief, 183, 185
Wilson, Gilbert L., 81
wolf, 10, 11–13, 14, 16, 17, 19, 21, 22, 25,
    26, 27, 29, 31, 33, 46, 60, 62, 74, 90, 91,
    100, 101, 109, 120, 123, 129, 130, 131,
    138, 144
Wolf-Chief, 81
Worsaae, J. J. A., 34

Xoloitzcuintli, 66, 149

Yorkshire, England, 39
Young, D. B., 125

Zagoskin, Lt. Lavrentiy A., 104